Rosie Waterland writes for the Mamamia Women's Network, covering all the important issues (mostly involving reality television and/or herself). Only 28 years old, she rose to fame in 2014 with her laugh-out-loud funny recaps of *The Bachelor*. She gets through most days by finding her own jokes particularly hilarious. This is her first book. To find out more about Rosie, go to rosiewaterland.com

 @RosieWaterland

 Rosie Waterland

CW00954234

the anti cool girl

rosie waterland

FOURTH ESTATE
An Imprint of HarperCollins*Publishers*

Some material in this book was originally published on
Mamamia Women's Network, mamamia.com.au
Giving head is the worst
mamamia.com.au/rogue/rosie-waterland-giving-head-is-the-worst
I have no freaking clue how banks work
mamamia.com.au/rogue/how-do-banks-work-you-dont-want-to-know
The moment I realised that I am not a functioning adult
mamamia.com.au/social/im-gen-y-and-i-dont-know-what-to-do-at-the-post-office
You'll be less of a woman if you have a caesarean
mamamia.com.au/parenting/what-are-your-push-values

Fourth Estate

An imprint of HarperCollins*Publishers*

First published in Australia in 2015
by HarperCollins*Publishers* Australia Pty Limited
ABN 36 009 913 517
harpercollins.com.au

HarperCollins*Publishers*
Level 13, 201 Elizabeth Street, Sydney NSW 2000, Australia
Unit D1, Apollo Drive, Rosedale, Auckland 0632, New Zealand
A 53, Sector 57, Noida, UP, India
1 London Bridge Street, London, SE1 9GF, United Kingdom
2 Bloor Street East, 20th floor, Toronto, Ontario M4W 1A8, Canada
195 Broadway, New York NY 10007, USA

National Library of Australia Cataloguing-in-Publication data:

Waterland, Rosie, author.
   The anti-cool girl / Rosie Waterland.
   978 1 4607 5064 3 (paperback)
   978 1 4607 0522 3 (ebook)
   Waterland, Rosie.
   Women – Australia – Conduct of life. Biography.
362.76092

Cover design by Darren Holt, HarperCollins Design Studio
Cover image by Rosie Waterland
Typeset in Bembo Std Regular by Kirby Jones
Printed and bound in Australia by Griffin Press
The papers used by HarperCollins in the manufacture of this book are natural, recyclable products made from wood grown in sustainable plantation forests. The fibre source and manufacturing processes meet recognised international environmental standards, and carry certification.

For Rhiannon, Tayla and Isabella.
She made each of us, and each of
us is an incredible woman.

Contents

You will be fed up before you've even left the womb.

Oh Rosie. Not even born yet, and already on the run. How exhausting. At a time when you should be concentrating on not growing an extra thumb, you're being tossed around in your mum's belly while she tries to jump-start an overheated hatchback by pushing it down a hill.

I feel for you, I really do. I know that it's 3am right now and all you want to do is sleep. But your parents are currently trying to escape the clutches of some violent bikie drug dealers, and they're having a little trouble getting the car started, so you may be up for a while.

You see, your dad, Tony, recently decided to take control of the family's financial future by securing a job in the petty drug-dealing industry. It makes sense – he already had extensive contacts from all the drugs that he and your mum, Lisa, had been, you know, taking. And with a three-year-old daughter at home (your older sister, Rhiannon), and another baby on the way (lucky you!), your parents needed to start bringing in some cash.

Now, I'm sure it seemed like a good idea at the time. I'm sure it seemed like a good idea right up until the moment your dad took all the drugs instead of selling them. Not surprisingly, the whole endeavour stopped seeming like a good idea when your dad found himself in a scary amount of debt to some very scary people, and they got word to him that his legs would be broken if he didn't pay back the cash. This is why you've now woken up at 3am to the muffled sounds of your parents trying to haul arse out of Balmain without being seen.

You truly are one lucky foetus.

You're meant to be born in four weeks, and despite the looming due-date, I know that you're still on the fence about whether or not you'd like to come out at all. I get it – even being a bun in a dangerous oven has to be better than whatever the hell is going on out there. Your instinct to bunker down in that womb and never come out is an understandable one.

But I'm afraid you have no choice, Rosie. Oh, you're going to fight it: you'll be three weeks late. You will rip your mum's junk to pieces on your way out (to this day, whenever you mention your birth, she gives you a look of horrified disdain that suggests you came out wielding an acid-coated machete). And, as a last-ditch effort to avoid what you somehow know is a less than ideal situation, you'll wrap the umbilical cord around your neck and stop breathing for over a minute.

You will make it abundantly clear; you're not interested in whatever the outside world is offering you.

But a slap on your wrinkly blue back will force air into your lungs and it'll be too late to go back in. You will be born, Rosie. Your mum will be screaming, your dad will be drunk out of his mind, and you will be born.

I wish I could tell you that things are going to be easy outside of that belly. I wish I could tell you that you aren't about to face years of confusion and chaos. I wish I could tell you that your parents won't abandon you, or that you'll never wet your pants in a supermarket while drunk.

But I can't tell you any of that. I can't promise that your life will be surrounded by a white picket fence, when I know that isn't true.

I can tell you this though, Rosie: although things are going to get much, much worse before they get better, they *will* get better. You're not always going to be an almost-human on the run from drug dealers. Things are going to change for you, I promise. You'll never learn to cook, but you will eventually grow into a semi-functional adult. So get comfortable (or at least try – the car is going to break down several more times tonight) and let me explain how this all goes down.

Your mum will be a sex worker, and you'll have no idea.

There is nothing more profoundly irritating than being peppered with questions about the strange man who sleeps in your mum's bed, when all you're trying to do is have fun at your fourth birthday party.

'But if he's not your dad, then who *is* he?'

How could I explain to this idiot that I didn't give a fuck who that man was? The more pressing issue was that this girl hurling questions in my face had decided to turn up at my fancy dress party in a costume that looked like some kind of unfortunate accident involving a fairy with sparkly diarrhoea.

I had tried to plan that damn party with an iron fist. If ever a four-year-old resembled a vicious and uncompromising dictator, it was me during the preparations for that celebration.

First of all, aside from mandatory family members, I wanted no females involved. Invitations would be offered *only* to the boys from my preschool (I was a proud early adopter of feminism).

Second, only I could dress as my hero and the one true god, Michelangelo the orange Ninja Turtle. Any embarrassing double-ups on that costume would result in immediate dismissal. Third, any girls who did attend, almost certainly against my wishes, needed to do so without any kind of tulle and/or sparkly wing arrangement.

Yes, it could be argued that I was being a tad controlling about the party situation (and also that I took being a tomboy to the extreme), but a couple of unfortunate bathroom mishaps in the preceding weeks meant I had some serious reputation repairing to do. Basically, I had embarrassed myself with shit – twice – and this party was a PR emergency.

The poo towel had come first.

I had been in the bathroom, doing my business, when I realised there was no toilet paper left. A mildly irritating occurrence for the experienced toilet-goer, but for someone still relatively early in her solo toilet career, I was completely thrown off kilter. I sat on the toilet, perplexed, for at least ten minutes. I was honestly at a loss. Then Rhiannon started banging on the door, telling me to hurry up in that threatening yet somehow legal way older siblings tend to do. She had friends over, and wanted to get back to whatever cool thing they were doing that I was never invited to join.

In a panic, I spotted a towel hanging on the rack. I knew what had to be done.

But just as I was completing the final wipe (making sure to keep going until there were no brown bits left – an important lesson from Mum), my sister barged through the door wanting to know what the hell was taking me so long.

I froze, pants around my ankles, poo towel in hand. Obviously, Rhiannon immediately told everyone, all her friends barged through the door to get a good look, and what little cred I had with the cool kids disappeared instantly.

Now, the poo towel was bad (although I learned nothing – if I've ever been to your house and you failed to provide me with toilet paper, then I'd be washing all towels in your immediate vicinity), but to be honest, I probably could have lived with the shame of getting caught in the moment, if it hadn't been for what happened a few days later.

Rhiannon's friends were over again, and because of some miracle that must have come directly from my hero Michelangelo himself, they needed an extra person to make up the numbers for some game they were playing. I had no idea how it worked, but from what I could gather, it basically involved running around the house lots and lots of times. I was just thrilled that kids three years older than me were finally recognising my potential, despite the fact I had just days earlier been involved in the embarrassing poo-towel incident. This complex running-around-the-house game was my chance to make up for past mistakes, and I was not going to blow it. Despite my complete lack of understanding of the point of the game, I ran around that house like my life fucking depended on it.

Until I felt a fart coming.

It stopped me cold. You see, farting is a dangerous game when you're still getting used to life without nappies. Each one can go either way, and while I had become fairly adept at recognising which ones would involve only air and which ones would need a toilet, I was still pretty inexperienced when it came to being in charge of my own bowel activities.

I needed a minute to concentrate and figure out exactly what was going on down there, but I could see the other kids ahead of me, and I wanted so badly to keep playing that I went for it.

I closed my eyes and pushed, praying that the gamble would pay off.

The shit that immediately started running down my leg was a fairly good indication that it hadn't.

At this point, I had two choices. I could go back inside before anybody saw, have my mum clean me up, and pretend like none of this had ever happened. But that would mean walking out on a game with the cool kids that I had been desperate to play since I first saw them running nonsensically around the house.

Alternatively, I could try and cover the mess as best I could, and keep playing until they realised I was the lame poo-towel girl and start to question why they had invited me out there in the first place. I was certain I was playing against the clock anyway, so it made sense to try and squeeze in as much time with these guys as I could.

I decided to go with option number two. Playing with my older sister and her friends was just too good an opportunity to walk out on, no matter what had just taken place in my underpants.

So I went into emergency clean-up mode. I figured if I could keep the situation contained to my undies, nobody would ever have to know. I used some leaves to wipe what had escaped down my leg, I scraped my hand on a tree to get rid of any evidence and I continued running around the house like nothing had happened.

It was Rhiannon who noticed first.

'What's that smell?' she said, looking at me suspiciously. Everybody came to a halt. 'Did you fart?'

'No!' I screamed, way too defensively for someone who currently had a massive shit smeared between her bum cheeks.

'Is that *poo*?' my sister asked, pointing at my leg.

I looked down. Damn. It was, in fact, poo. My emergency clean-up and containment plan had not yielded successful results.

So that's how I found myself, for the second time in three days, standing in the bathroom while being laughed at by the cool kids. I couldn't understand why Mum had left the door wide open, but I was so paralysed by embarrassment that I couldn't bring myself to say anything. I will say this now, though: if ever there's a time for privacy, it's when you're bent over the sink while your mum wipes shit from your arse with a wet rag from the kitchen.

So, given the unfortunate and embarrassing poo-related events of the preceding weeks, you can understand why I considered this birthday party my opportunity to show Rhiannon's friends that I was back on track, you know, life-wise.

That's why I had organised the party with a miniature iron fist, and that's why I was so pissed off that I was now face-to-face with a pink human pastry puff, asking me to explain my mother's sleeping arrangements.

I knew Scott was my mum's friend. I knew he was a taxi driver. I knew that when we moved into his house, there weren't enough rooms for everybody, so he and my mum had to share. I knew that when I sometimes saw them naked it was just because sometimes grown-ups sleep naked. I couldn't understand why it was so damn hard for this idiot standing in front of me to comprehend.

Doesn't everybody's mum sleep naked with her friend Scott the Taxi Driver?

It was perfectly acceptable to me that theirs was a friends-only arrangement. But I guess you don't question that stuff when you're just trying to get through life without shitting your pants more than twice in a week.

How could I possibly have known that Mum and Scott met when he used to drive her home after her long shifts as a sex worker? How could I possibly have known that on those 3am taxi rides, he had fallen in love with her ridiculous beauty and decided he could save her? How could I possibly have known that he moved us into his house, and that's why we didn't live with the girls near the brothel anymore? (Come to think of it, how could I have possibly known that was a brothel?) How could I possibly have known that when my mum accepted his offer of a boob job, she also accepted his offer of a cheap home for her children so she could stop selling her body and go back to the far less lucrative profession of nursing?

All I knew was that we lived with my mum's friend Scott, and they shared a room because there wasn't enough space.

Had I been faced with this human tulle-diarrhoea explosion later in life, I would have been able to give her cake-smeared face a far more detailed answer. But in that moment, dressed as Michelangelo the orange Ninja Turtle at my fourth birthday party, trying desperately to make up for some embarrassing toilet mishaps from my recent past, I was in no position to tell that girl anything.

It was only much later that I was able to piece together some of the details, but it's still difficult to understand how a girl went from an exclusive private school on the North Shore to the parking lot of a brothel in Wagga Wagga.

My mum was abandoned the moment she was born. Her mother was sixteen, terrified and sent away to another state to give birth in secret. The moment my mum came into the world, she was wrapped in a blanket and ushered out of the room, the exhausted teenage girl who had just delivered her not even allowed to see her face. She did name her, though: Katherine.

Within days, Katherine was adopted by an upper-middle-class couple that couldn't have children of their own. They already had two adopted sons, but desperately wanted a girl. They renamed their new daughter Lisa, and just like that, Katherine had been erased.

But even in her 'new' life, her 'better' life, mum was always filled with so much sorrow. It's almost like something in her knew she had been Katherine before she had been Lisa, and she couldn't handle the pain that came with knowing her birth mother hadn't wanted her.

As long as I've known her, my mum has felt abandoned and alone, and from what I can tell, she always did.

Raised on Sydney's leafy and affluent North Shore, my mum, along with her two adopted brothers, attended some of the best private schools in the country. Every opportunity was afforded to her, but she just couldn't seem to stay out of trouble. She was a 'bad girl'. At least, as bad as you can be when you're a privileged white kid from Turramurra. I think there was a bit of smoking behind the toilets and kissing boys and sneaking out after 8pm. That sort of scandalous thing.

She was moved to a country boarding school, but after she was expelled, her parents grew increasingly frustrated. This was not the girl they had signed up for. She was fiercely intelligent, popular and creatively gifted, but she was also incredibly self-destructive. She spent some time at secretarial school, some time at nursing school, but mostly she just wanted to party with her friends. She would later be diagnosed with Bipolar Disorder, but at the time, everyone just considered her an insufferable, rebellious teen.

Her parents kicked her out of the house, and she immediately went on to make a series of ridiculously bad life decisions. The first of which was my dad, Tony.

After meeting in a share-house, they quickly became inseparable. He was eleven years older than her, and married at the time they met. He had no job, drank heavily and did a lot of drugs. All qualities that clearly scream 'good catch'. After leaving his wife to be with Mum, he started controlling and abusing her almost immediately. My mum worked as a nursing assistant to support them both, then became pregnant with Rhiannon. I'm assuming at that point, she was the only twenty-year-old alumna from Ravenswood School for Girls living in a share-house bedroom and pregnant with an abusive junkie's baby.

Things got worse when she finally connected with her birth mother. Theirs is an incredible story – the kind that should have ended like a quirky Nora Ephron film, but instead ended like *Requiem for a Dream*, except with Darth Vader telling Luke he's his father instead of the double-dildo scene.

My mum had always known she was adopted; it wasn't kept secret in her family. So as soon as she could put her name on a list to try and connect with her birth mother, she did it. She had been following the work of a woman called Kate, an academic who worked with local adoption support groups and had written a book about women who had given up their children during the fifties, sixties and seventies. My mum had the book in her nightstand, and fantasised about her own mother being one of the women featured in it. How incredible would it be to find out your adoption was coerced, and your mother had actually wanted you all along?

Just a few weeks after registering her name, my mum got the call. Her birth mother had been located, and she *had* been in Mum's nightstand the entire time. Kate, the academic and adoption rights advocate whose work my mum had been following, was in actual fact her birth mother.

And it turns out, though they may have tried, my adopted grandparents hadn't managed to erase all trace of Katherine the day they renamed my mother Lisa. There, on the front page of Kate's book, was a dedication:

'For Katherine.'

My mum immediately assumed that her adoption had been forced. This woman had dedicated her life's work to sharing the stories of those who had been heartbreakingly affected by the adoption process – her book was dedicated to the daughter she had lost. To her! The part inside of my mum that had always felt abandoned was desperate to know that it hadn't been her mother's choice.

But it *had* been her choice.

Kate, a straightforward and often harsh woman, told my mum that while she had struggled with the loss of her daughter, she still knew it was the best thing for both of them at the time.

Their relationship was strained from that point, disappointment on both sides simmering tensions.

My mum had hoped for a warm and loving woman who had always been desperately looking for the baby that was stolen from her. Instead, she found a woman who was cold, overly academic and very open about the fact she had wanted the adoption.

Kate had hoped for a strong, independent and driven feminist, hopefully at university and on her way to incredible things. Instead she found an unmarried twenty-year-old with a kid, a woman who liked to drink and do drugs and was living with an abusive alcoholic eleven years her senior.

Neither of them was particularly impressed with the other.

They tried having a relationship. Kate even found my mother an apartment and helped her escape my dad, a plan that fell to pieces when my dad moved in anyway and within days had threatened the landlord with a gun. As was his way.

Far from the relationship they had hoped for, mother and daughter continued to confound and exasperate each other.

Then, during a fight, Kate told my mother that if abortion had been available to her back in 1963, she would have taken that option.

It's a story I've heard my mum tell through drunken tears many times. As someone who wasn't even born when all this went down, I have the benefit and the curse of only being able to piece together a narrative from what I've been told by various characters who were part of the action. I don't know how angry the two of them were; I don't know if voices were raised. I don't know what kind of infuriating thing my mother had done to upset Kate, or if she had done anything at all. But I do know that Kate said it, and that it broke something in my mum that could never be repaired.

Forget being erased, now it was like Katherine had never existed at all.

My mum had hoped that finding her birth mother would melt away the feelings of loneliness and abandonment. Instead, she just felt the darkness cement itself in her body. A darkness that would lead to alcoholism, drugs, suicide attempt after suicide attempt, and eventually, in a bizarre 'circle of life' type scenario, the state removal of her own children.

Her adopted and birth mothers had both given up on her. The loneliness she had been afraid of her whole life was now a heavy reality in the pit of her stomach. So when my dad, the only person who had stuck around so far, suggested she try her hand at sex work to support the family, she did it.

After Dad had his little firearm run-in with the landlord, and unsuccessfully tried to be a drug dealer, we were stuck in hiding, living near his parents in Tumut, a small country town in the west of New South Wales. My mum decorated cakes and Easter eggs for the local bakery, but with two kids (I had conveniently made my appearance by this stage) and an abusive partner with drinking and drug habits to support, she needed a lot more than bakery-level money.

She looked in the paper and saw that there were some 'places' in Wagga Wagga that she could go. Wagga was the closest thing Tumut had to a city. It was about an hour away, and where married Tumut couples went when they wanted a fancy night on the town. It was also a popular destination for long-haul truck drivers, who used it as a place to stop and get … some.

My mum hooked up with one of the local brothels and got to work. Just a few years earlier she had been getting in trouble for not polishing her school shoes.

I once asked her about the first time — about the first client she ever worked with. She said they were in a tiny motel room. He was short and bald, and asked her to rub coconut oil all over his shiny head as some kind of sick, slick foreplay. She said the oil stank, and as he was thrusting into her, it took everything she had not to vomit. When it was over, she couldn't believe what she had done, and spent the whole night trying to wash the smell of the oil off her hands. Even though it was twenty-five years later, she still cried a little when she told me she would never, ever forget that smell.

But as awful as it was, she had children to feed, and a violent partner to keep liquored up. So every weekend, my mum would drive out to Wagga and make as much money as she could.

Then something in her clicked. She realised she was beautiful, and educated, and that working in a brothel for truck drivers in fucking Wagga was way below her league. She decided that if she was going to have to sell herself, she was going to be smart about it. So she moved back to Sydney and set herself up as a high-class escort.

With some financial independence, she was able to break things off with my dad. They fought over custody of us for a while, but it could be argued that in a fight between an unemployed alcoholic and a 22-year-old escort, there aren't really any winners.

We ended up with Mum, who had somehow ended up with Scott the Taxi Driver – the first of many men she hoped would save her. She had become excellent at using her very specific set of skills to work with men. Even after she stopped having sex for money, men would always be like a job in her life. A way to survive. Each man was a shift she had to get through, and one day, if she worked hard enough, and played her cards just right, she'd finally be able to clock off. Scott the Taxi Driver was just her latest shift.

But I knew none of that at my fourth birthday party. I didn't know the very sad and bizarre sequence of events that had led to my mum sharing a bed with her 'friend' Scott the Taxi Driver. I didn't know that when she got sick of sharing that bed, we would end up as far away as Hawaii. I didn't know that there would be many more embarrassing poo-related disasters in my life to come, and this party was just the start of my quest to impress the cool kids. All I knew was that I didn't want to be answering that damn question from a girl dressed as fairy diarrhoea. And even if I had wanted to explain my mother's sleeping arrangements, I didn't know how.

So, I looked her up and down, and making absolutely no attempt to hide the disdain on my face, I said, 'Your disgusting dress is ruining my party. Please leave and come back as a Ninja Turtle.'

You will be a Houso kid.

When you find yourself sitting on top of a dirt mound, waiting until nobody's looking so the girl from up the street can lick your special place, you really start to take stock of your life. Yes, I was only five, but I was definitely having some kind of serious existential crisis at that exact, confusing moment.

It was my need to impress that had got me into this mess, I knew that much. My need to impress my perfect, beautiful, calculating eight-year-old sister, who thought the whole thing was fucking hilarious.

Rhiannon was pretty horrendous to me. I was certain her behaviour qualified her for some kind of psychological program that tested her facial expressions when shown pictures of dead piglets. Let's just say she was walking a very fine line between future CEO and future serial killer. (She ended up a working single mum of two, which I think takes just as much precision and brutality as both those positions.)

She locked me in cupboards, convinced me Pennywise the Clown from Stephen King's *It* wanted to kill me, busted me when I tried to hide my wet underpants behind the washing machine. Standard big-sister stuff that I obviously assumed was happening only to me and would eventually be turned into an epic film focussing on my brave survival, which I would write, direct and star in.

I considered my relationship with her to be material for my moving yet witty Oscars speech, which would be called 'pitch perfect' by the press. She considered her relationship with me as nothing but an opportunity for hilarious daily sadism.

And I worshipped her.

She was just so perfect, so cool. All the boys loved her, and all the girls wanted to be her. She was so beautiful and mean, and understood how to strike that elusive balance between treating people badly and having them desperately want to impress you. She was just instinctively popular – a skill I neither had nor understood.

She knew which clothes to pick out at Best and Less to make it look like she had stepped out of a Mariah Carey video (denim shorts, hat with a sunflower on it). She understood which songs on Rage were cool and which ones weren't. She liked New Kids on the Block when I was still taking my plastic Fisher Price record player with me to the bath.

Rhiannon knew that I wanted her to teach me how to be a cool kid. She also knew that as long as I didn't realise that reading RL Stine's *Goosebumps* alone in my room was lame, I never would be. I was freckle-faced, desperate and clueless, and she had the power to get me to do whatever she wanted.

So when Leslie, the weird girl who lived in the apartments up the street, asked us if we dared her to lick one of our fannies, Rhiannon immediately replied, 'Yes! Rosie does!'

And that was how she planned to torture me that day.

I gave her a look that sat somewhere between, 'Please don't make me do this with the weird girl who always smells like cheese,' and, 'But seriously, if I do this will you let me hang out with you for the rest of the day?'

I was the worst kind of desperado.

We spent some time haggling over terms. It would be one quick lick. I wouldn't have to take my undies off, only move them to the side. And we would do it on top of Ayers Rock, the giant dirt mound behind our house that was so high, nobody would be able to see what we were up to.

There was also a strict confidentiality clause. Once the deed was done, it was at Defcon 5–level secrecy. I had insisted on that terminology. I had no idea what it meant, but I'd heard it on TV, where it was always said by an army man and it always sounded serious. And I was the smartest of the three of us by far, which everybody knew, so they didn't question it.

What bothered me, though, was that nobody was questioning this Leslie chick. She had mentioned that she could do this weird thing, Rhiannon's face had filled with glee and the operation was in full swing before I even had time to check if my current underwear had skidmarks.

I pulled Rhiannon aside and raised my concerns. Why did this girl want to do this? How did she even know that licking your fanny special place was a thing? Did we really want to trust someone who lived in the apartments and smelled like cheese?

'Rosanna,' she said, rolling her eyes as if I'd just asked her to compete in a poetry competition with me (which I definitely hadn't just days earlier), 'Just do it.'

I was so weak-willed that one eye-roll was literally all it took. Rhiannon was like some kind of cool magician. One strategic sigh from her could send you into a tailspin of popularity-questioning confusion. I had no choice. I had to do it. I had to let the cheese girl lick my special place.

So there I was, sitting on top of the dirt mound, stalling until the exact moment I had to move my undies aside. Rhiannon was sitting next to me, already hysterically laughing, and Leslie was crouched in front of me, trying to calmly convince me that none of this was a big deal.

Just a year earlier I had been living in Hawaii, thrilled that being in America meant I was one step closer to Hollywood. How had I ended up a Houso kid, with the cheese girl's face three inches from my vag?

My mind was questioning everything. My identity, the
universe, why I still wasn't allowed to have showers instead of
baths even though I was five and writing a screenplay. *How had I
come to be in this place?*

It was all because my mum had tried to pull off a Pretty
Woman.

After living with Scott the Taxi Driver for a while, she
decided the boob job he had gifted her was being wasted on her
nursing gig, so she took those spectacular new implants and went
back to charging dudes to touch them. Scott the Taxi Driver, the
man she shared a bed with even though he was definitely just her
friend, was no more.

John the Navy Man was one of Mum's clients, and the man
she selected to be her Richard Gere. He was a US Navy sailor
from Hawaii looking for some fun; instead, he found a beautiful
call girl who he could rescue. And just like that, John the Navy
Man married Mum, told her she could stop working that icky
job and whisked her away to take care of her.

(Oh, and I'm sure she was the first call girl he ever went to
see, and he *definitely* only did it out of peer pressure. Romance,
fairytales etc etc.)

Before I knew what the hell was what, my sister and I were
on a plane to Hawaii. We moved into a Navy compound and
started school. I found a palm tree out the front that I could
practise hitting with my Ninja Turtle sword. We made friends

and chased geckos and frogs around the backyard. My dad recorded all the cartoon theme songs off the Australian *Saturday Disney* and sent them to me on a tape, so I could set up an arena in the living room and practise my performance skills. I thought things were pretty damn great.

Then came talk of a transfer to Wisconsin, which my mother accurately deduced was not Hawaii. And just as quickly as we had come, we left. One day we just got on a plane and flew back to Sydney. We had only been in Honolulu for ten months.

I'm fairly certain my mum just wanted a holiday. We never saw John the Navy Man again, and my mum never sold her body again. Which meant we had no money, no man and no place to go.

It was time for us to become a Houso family.

I'm sure most Australian public housing is really quite lovely. But there can also be certain pockets that are cesspools of poverty, crime and a ridiculous amount of unprotected sex, which often results in lots of scary gangs made up of children without shoes.

In order to try and stop these cesspools from occurring, Houso homes were often built into regular neighbourhoods, as a kind of 'regular people buffer' for those of us who couldn't be trusted when all lumped together. Diluting the problem, if you will.

We were not diluted with a regular neighbourhood.

My mum, Rhiannon and I were placed in Smurf Village, one of the only exclusively Houso neighbourhoods in New South Wales. Also called Lego Land (or sometimes the Ghetto), it had been named as such because all the houses were identical, connected and blue. The townhouses literally looked like giant blue Lego blocks that had been snapped together in long rows.

The Ghetto nickname was thrown around because the neighbourhood was also completely closed off. There was only one road in, and that road led to every corner of Smurf Village. It was like one of those gated communities that rich families live in on TV, except we didn't need a gate, because anybody who didn't live there was too scared to drive in anyway. And our houses certainly weren't as nice.

Smurf Village was gloriously located in North Ryde, with Macquarie Shopping Centre on one side and the El Rancho Bar and Bistro on the other.

After being lugged around to countless shitty homes in our short, little lives, everywhere from country New South Wales to Honolulu Navy compounds, Rhiannon and I felt like we had landed in a cosmopolitan paradise. I was relieved to finally be exposed to the culture that I felt like I deserved.

Macquarie Centre was like our Mecca. There was an ice-skating rink, a McDonald's *and* a KFC, a Woolworths ... even a play land made to look like an African safari. And if you were really lucky and it was a special occasion, your mum would buy you a dress from Grace Bros instead of Big W, but you had to make sure you told everyone so they would know the difference. You also had to keep the tags on, which I didn't exactly understand, but I did notice that I usually only wore a Grace Bros dress once and then my mum took it away.

The El Rancho was the epitome of Smurf Village bogan class. There was a bar for the grown-ups and a bistro for the kids, and the men would put on their best white jeans and Maseur sandals if it was after 6pm. The sign out the front made it look like a Spanish resort, and pulling into that car park meant you were definitely getting chicken nuggets and chips for dinner. And the lemonade was always pink, because when you went to the El Rancho, you did things right.

Yep, Smurf Village was smack bang in the middle of North Ryde's cultural epicentre. I actually couldn't believe how many rungs up the ladder I had managed to climb. And being within walking distance of Macquarie and the El Rancho wasn't even the best part. The best part was that Smurf Village was overrun with kids. All kids our age, and all with parents whose concept of supervision was telling them to be home by dark, and not to talk to the mentally disabled guy who told us that if we came back to his house he would give us Kit Kats.

It was heavenly mayhem. We would run around in giant packs, chasing each other in epic games of Home 44, or climbing the massive pile of dirt and rubble that was apparently meant to end up a park but would eventually just be christened Ayers Rock. Rhiannon and I were officially part of a gang of shoeless Houso kids, and it was all because our mum had made a failed attempt at pulling off a Pretty Woman.

People who drove past our compound on the way to Macquarie probably considered us trash, and the police who did the rounds in their cars each night shook their heads when we said we didn't know where our parents were.

But we had fun together. Most of the kids who lived there had seen, or were still seeing, some messed-up stuff in their short, little lives, and playing Home 44 until ten o'clock at night made us feel normal.

Mitchell and Marcus lived across the street. Their dad was a heroin addict who only turned up occasionally, and their mum beat the absolute shit out of them for the most bizarre reasons, like closing the door too loudly or knocking over a pot plant.

There was a Guatemalan family next door, who I could have sworn had about twenty-seven people living in that one tiny house. Nina was our age, and when we walked to Macquarie, her parents couldn't even afford to give her money for a soft serve.

Tim lived a few houses down from us, and the police were at his place all the time. When our rabbit had babies, we gave him two of them, and he drowned them both in his pool.

Then, of course, there was Leslie, the weird girl who smelled like cheese and lived in the Houso apartments, which was the only thing worse than living in a blue Lego house. I went to her apartment once, motivated mostly by a sense of curiosity and the promise of dinner. When her mum dropped a plate of half-defrosted fish fingers in front of us and went back to watching *Wheel of Fortune*, I was mortified. I felt like I needed to stage some kind of intervention. I wanted to put my hand on hers and ask if there was anything I could do, and maybe gently hint at the cheese odour situation. Then she said we should go to her bedroom and act out the sex scenes from *Days of Our Lives*.

Yep. Every kid at Smurf Village had obviously seen some messed-up stuff.

I tried to focus on those sad, defrosted fish fingers while sitting on top of Ayers Rock. I was hoping they would conjure up some kind of sympathy in me that would enable me to get through this so-called quick lick. 'She's so much worse off than you!' I was telling myself. 'You are such a generous spirit for doing this. And you'll get to hang out with Rhiannon for the rest of the day!'

I took a deep breath, reached down, pulled my undies aside and gave the go-ahead. 'Do it,' I said, suddenly remembering that sometimes my fanny smelled bad and praying this wasn't one of those times. *'Just do it.'*

Leslie bent down, gave me a quick lick, and that was it. The whole thing lasted less than a second. Leslie burst into hysterical laughter. I immediately looked to Rhiannon for approval. She had demanded I do the thing and I had done the thing! I was sure this would gain me some respect, at least for the day.

'Oh my god,' Rhiannon said in disbelief. 'I can't believe you did it. Ewwww! I can't believe you did it!' She got up, sprinted down the side of Ayers Rock and headed straight to Nina's house, no doubt to spread the word that I had spread my legs.

That was not how I had anticipated the operation turning out. I pushed Leslie over, told her she smelled like cheese and went back to my room to plan my next Oscars speech. This one was going to be fucking good.

By about six o'clock that evening, Mum knew everything, and she was not impressed. She may have been living in the Ghetto, but she grew up on the North Shore, damn it, and this was not how children were supposed to behave. She didn't like the little boy who had drowned our rabbits in the pool, and she definitely now had a problem with the girl who had licked my fanny. She considered us fish out of water, like a reverse *Beverly Hillbillies*, and we were obviously better people than this.

It didn't help that every so often my adopted grandparents would come to visit, turning up in their fancy car, looking horrified and politely refusing to make contact with any foreign surface. But they would never stay long, and when they left, as much as my mum didn't want to believe it, they would take the North Shore with them.

We did belong at Smurf Village. We were part of Lego Land. We lived in the Ghetto.

And nothing made that more obvious than when my dad started to show up.

Your friends will find a dead body in the bush, and it will be your dad.

'There's a dead guy! *A dead guy!*'

We all stopped what we were doing immediately. It doesn't matter how well you're doing in your game of Pog, when someone says there's a dead guy in the park, you drop what you're doing and you pay attention.

It was a weekend at Smurf Village, which meant the shoeless child gangs were out in force. We pretty much spent days off school just roaming around, teasing people who lived in the apartments and playing whatever Rhiannon had dictated was the cool thing to be playing that week.

Ayers Rock had finally been removed and replaced with a park, which meant most kids hung out down there and snuck into the bush that ran alongside it. But Rhiannon had decided on Pog that day, so I was sitting with her in our driveway, along with Nina, who didn't own any Pogs but took whatever chance she could get to escape a house filled with twenty-seven Guatemalan relatives.

Since Rhiannon had unusually allowed me to participate in her game in a way that – so far – had nothing to do with torturing me and/or decimating my dignity, I obviously proceeded to self-destruct in a spectacular fashion. I was always so desperate to play with the cool kids, but once I got there, I had very little concept of how to keep my shit together.

I started trying to convince the girls to help me produce a play I was writing about homeless kids, who survive by stealing cups of noodles from the supermarket. I would obviously be the star, playing a beautiful and brilliant Olympic-trained gymnast who had run away from home because her stepmother was jealous of her starring role on *Saved by the Bell*. I would also play any other role that had any kind of dramatic arc or involved any kind of acting talent. I basically just needed the girls to be warm bodies that I could bounce breathtaking monologues off.

And just as Rhiannon was starting to question whether getting her hands on my Pog collection was worth having to be in my immediate vicinity for an extended period, we started hearing the screams coming from the park.

A bunch of kids came running out of the bush, their hysteria gathering momentum as they got closer to the street.

'We saw it! We *poked* it! There's a dead guy in his undies!'

Kids started coming out of nooks and crannies all over the place. This was big news. Some believed it, some didn't, but all of them wanted to at least look. I mean, it was a *dead guy*. This may have been the Ghetto, but even kids like us hadn't seen anything like *that*. It was too good to miss, and it was decided that we would all head down together.

Rhiannon and I exchanged a knowing glance. We both immediately suspected it was him. I had that sick feeling in my stomach that I got whenever he was around. It was like my sixth sense for dysfunctionality, and right now it was telling me what none of the other kids knew: my dad was the dead guy in the bush they were poking with sticks.

Everyone ran excitedly towards him. Rhiannon and I walked slowly behind, both taking advantage of the short time we had left in which it could still be someone else. We didn't talk to each other. We didn't look at each other. We just walked silently across the park, following the sounds of the barefoot child gang, screaming like they were in a haunted funhouse.

My stomach got worse the closer we got. By the time we caught up with the gaggle of kids, their excitement had reached fever pitch, and my stomach had turned to poison in my body, a poison made of unrelenting toxic butterflies. My sixth sense never lied; I knew it had to be him.

Rhiannon and I pushed through the crowd and looked down at the exciting attraction in front of us.

The man was on his back in the dirt. He was wearing only underwear and a filthy white t-shirt. No shoes. No possessions. His skin was glowing red from having been roasted in the sun for what looked like hours. His eyes were closed and his body was still.

As the kids around us squealed and giggled and dared each other to touch it, the universe for Rhiannon and me shrank to include only us. I swallowed and looked at her, trying not to vomit, the toxic butterflies threatening to crack my body wide open. She looked back at me, tears in her eyes and panic on her face.

The universe out there was one where we frustrated each other and fought with each other. She couldn't stand my clueless quest to fit in (which, for some reason, had involved way too many toilet mishaps), and I couldn't understand her reluctance to accept me, or her unwillingness to try reading as a recreational activity.

But in this universe, in this moment, we were in sync. As we stood there and locked on each other's eyes, everything around us was a blur, and we understood each other better and loved each other more than anyone else ever would.

My sixth sense *had* been right. The man in the dirt was our dad.

I wasn't surprised that I had known. I'd had plenty of time to hone the unique sense that caused me to vomit whenever he was nearby. Dad had started turning up at Smurf Village not long after we'd moved in.

One morning I woke up before everyone else and headed down to the kitchen, hoping to hack into the chocolate part of the Neapolitan ice-cream before anyone noticed. I'm sorry, but why does Neapolitan ice-cream even exist? If I can find one person who eats the strawberry part and leaves the vanilla and chocolate parts, then I can guarantee you I've found the person responsible for whatever murders are currently unsolved in your town.

Just as I was getting to the kitchen, I saw a human-shaped lump stumble over the back fence and fall to the ground with an undignified thud. My stomach churned. I stood at the back door and watched as he lay on the ground, the open bottle of scotch he had somehow managed to hold onto while jumping the fence now leaking all over him. When he realised the bottle had emptied, he started trying to scoop the spilled liquid from his body into his mouth, while simultaneously trying (and failing) to get up off the ground. It was like watching a turtle stuck on its back, if the turtle had a drinking problem and was scaring the shit out of his six-year-old daughter.

I abandoned the ice-cream plan, went back to my room and pretended I was still asleep.

Another time I was playing the star in my youth group's nativity play. 'The Star' was a part I had invented when some other bitch beat me to the role of Mary. I basically just had to hold up a star made of yellow cardboard for the entire play, but I insisted I do it in the middle of the stage, standing on a chair, while wearing enough glittered clothing to make Liza Minnelli think I was tacky. I was sure it was going to be the defining moment of my acting career so far, and probably launch me as a wunderkind prodigy in the local North Ryde theatre scene. Instead, right before the show, someone in the crowd told me a man was walking around saying he was Rosanna's dad. I threw up, and spent all my time on stage trying to spot a stumbling drunk man in the audience.

My life started to revolve around hoping he wouldn't show up where I was, and throwing up whenever he did. 'Rosanna, there's a man here who says he's your dad. Um, does he drink a lot, sweetie?' was the kind of sentence that sent my body into total lockdown. My stomach would drop, the toxic butterflies coursing through every inch of my veins. My brain would swirl and my breathing would slow, until my body was no longer made of blood, but millions of poisonous pairs of wings. Then my stomach would make an executive decision on behalf of my brain, which by that point had usually decided it couldn't deal and was going to sit this one out. The toxic butterflies would be very suddenly and very forcefully ejected. Which really just means I would vomit, violently. Usually all over myself, but often on whichever unfortunate person happened to be standing in my pretty impressive projectile range.

My dad was unpredictable because he had nowhere to go. He didn't live in Sydney, so when he was there, he would just wander around, drunk and hoping to run into Rhiannon or me. Home for him was actually still in Tumut, exactly where my mum had left him a couple of years before. After she stopped bankrolling his life with her body, he was forced to move in with his dad, who was also an alcoholic. Theirs was a very sad scotch-soaked bachelor pad, and their shared life was like a Chuck Lorre sitcom directed by Lars von Trier.

Since Tumut is hours from Sydney, I honestly don't know how he got to North Ryde each time. But I do know that unless my mum let him stay with us, he was essentially homeless while he was there.

The few times she did give him a chance, he took it and soaked it in so much alcohol-fuelled disaster that it became harder and harder for her to offer him a place to stay. He would forget he had taken Rhiannon and me places, and leave us waiting for hours to be picked up. He would collapse in the middle of busy streets, take us to the pub and forget we were there, get on the wrong buses and end up stranded on the outskirts of Sydney in the middle of the night. Just your general, incredibly dysfunctional, alcoholic dad kind of stuff.

All of it was pretty difficult for two girls under ten to deal with (there really is not a lot you can do when your dad insists that you jaywalk through busy traffic, then proceeds to pass out halfway across the road), but for me, none of it brought on the toxic butterflies like the shoplifting.

My dad did not like using money to pay for things. It probably had something to do with the fact he generally didn't *have* money to pay for things. But it wasn't just about desperation or lack of funds with him. I really think he just took a weird Winona-like pleasure in the act itself, and would pick up the most bizarre, nonsensical objects just for the sake of it. I can't count the number of times he was escorted out of shopping centres by security, Rhiannon and I following behind with our heads down, only to find he'd taken a pair of teddy bear glasses, or the buttons off a shirt. And he did get caught, *every time*. Because the only thing worse than being a shoplifter is being a terrible shoplifter, and the only thing worse than being a terrible shoplifter is being a terrible shoplifter who is also drunk.

I didn't quite understand his considerable lack of talent as a thief, until I saw him, barely able to stand, shoving a shirt inside his pants. We were shopping in Wagga Wagga for the day, my sister and I left to wander around with Dad while our grandpa went to do whatever it is that grandpas do (I honestly don't know … getting fitted for beige pants?). We walked past a store and Dad saw a shirt that he liked. He stumbled inside, pulling me along with him. Rhiannon, who seemed to sense that something illegal was about to go down, made herself scarce, so as not to be implicated in any criminal proceedings. But alas, I was still young and naïve, and not entirely aware of my father's career as the world's worst criminal.

He took the shirt off the rack and started to stuff it inside his pants. I'm not sure if he thought he was being incognito, but he reeked of alcohol, was having trouble balancing and had two little girls with him who looked terrified, so he was pretty much in the spotlight from the second he walked in the store. This was not the stealth operation I think he thought it was.

Feeling the toxic butterflies about to explode out of my mouth in the form of breakfast, I tried my best to give my dad an alibi, or at least some kind of reasonable motive. I looked around the store and said, as loud as I could, 'So, you're just holding on to that shirt so when we come back later to buy it, nobody will have taken it, right?'

He looked at me, a little stunned, like his skills were so incredible he couldn't believe that I had just seen him stuff a shirt down his pants.

'Um … yeah, Sannie. That's it. I don't want anyone to take it,' he said. Then we quickly left the store, Rhiannon being careful not to walk alongside us until she could be sure she was no longer near the crime scene.

Next stop was the pub, where Dad bought a much needed beer and Rhiannon and I shared a pink lemonade. We needed to wait for Grandpa to finish his important Wagga business (again, I don't know … shopping for World War II books?), and it was just as we were sitting patiently in the beer garden that a man came over to our table and started aggressively taking our picture.

'Thief! Thief!' he screamed, aiming the camera in our faces. Dad was too dazed to comprehend what the hell was going on, but I knew: his Wagga crime spree had not gone to plan.

Everyone in the pub was looking at us, and this guy just wouldn't stop. He was the owner of the store Dad had taken the shirt from, and he was furious. He kept yelling at us and taking our picture until the police arrived. I've always wondered what happened to that roll of film. What do you do with twenty-six photos of a confused-looking man and two little girls crying? I threw up, and Dad was put in the back of a paddy wagon. This was well before mobile phones existed outside of movies, so I have no idea how they found Grandpa, but they did. The last thing I remember is sitting in the front of the wagon, looking back through the peephole at Dad, nothing but a sad, black outline in the back of a police van.

Mum did what she could for Dad when he randomly turned up at Smurf Village, drunk and with nowhere to go. One morning I woke to find him sleeping on a mattress on the floor of my room, with Mum sitting next to him, stroking his face and crying, begging him not to die. I threw up in my bed. After that, she would usually leave blankets out for him and let him stay in the garage, as long as he promised to be gone before we woke up, because, 'Rosanna gets so stressed.'

But I always knew when he was around. It was my sixth sense. Barely out of kindergarten, my Dad-radar was a finely tuned machine. I could determine how close he was by a mere rumble in my belly. The fluttering of a thousand poisonous wings would always tell me, and at that moment, they were telling me that he was dead. Which is why I was surprised when he moaned. As Rhiannon and I were standing there, frozen, looking down at our dead dad in the dirt, he moaned.

Let me tell you something: nothing will ever terrify a bunch of kids more than telling them they're standing in front of a dead body, only to have that dead body make a sound. For all their tough talk and gangster bravado, I've never seen twenty-five kids run away faster than they did when my dead dad started moaning in the dirt.

He was alive, obviously. Very, very drunk, but alive.

Rhiannon and I turned around and ran back up to the house. I was silent, she was hysterical. She told Mum, who called an ambulance. When it arrived, it felt like every human being in north-west Sydney came to watch the spectacle. As two paramedics walked him to the gurney, a kid came running out of the bush with a plastic bag. It was Dad's stuff.

The kids, a lot less terrified now that it was just some drunk guy and not a zombie, chased the ambulance as it drove up the hill and out of our compound, and once it had disappeared into the distance, everyone just kind of dispersed and went back to what they had been doing. The excitement was over; the man in the dirt was gone.

I went to the bathroom, put my head over the toilet, and pushed every last toxic butterfly out of my stomach.

Jesus will propose to your sister, and not you. Dick.

My sister got to marry Jesus and I didn't.

Just like all the other boys in Smurf Village, he liked her and not me. And I have to say, given his alleged noble qualities, I was a little surprised that he turned out to be just another guy who ignored the smart, awkward girl and went straight for the beautiful one. (Also, I would end up having a very brief period in my early twenties, right after my freckles faded, and just before I gained a lot of weight, in which I was considered quite attractive. So suck on that, Jesus.)

Rhiannon's proposal came about rather quickly, as far as rushed romances go. I'm not sure if you could call it an *arranged* marriage, but my mum certainly facilitated the proceedings. Basically, one day she decided that we were Mormons. I'm not sure exactly how it happened, but I like to think Mum looked at the eager, sensibly dressed young men holding their Bibles who had just knocked on our door, shrugged her shoulders and said, 'Yeah. Alright.'

A few months later Rhiannon was put in a white dress, shoved down the aisle and dunked under water, thus cementing her love connection with the big man himself.

As usual, I watched from the sidelines, not surprised that yet another man had chosen her over me. I was probably about seven, which would have put her at about ten, and even then I knew there was a huge disparity in our looks. She had gorgeous olive skin and those wide-set alien eyes that were becoming popular in the early '90s thanks to the likes of Kate Moss. I inherited my dad's Irish skin, was covered in dark freckles and my eyes were small, grey and unremarkable. I wasn't unfortunate-looking by any means – in fact, I was quite pretty – but nobody was stopping me in the street asking me to do Kmart commercials.

Rhiannon was constantly stopped in the street and asked to do Kmart commercials.

But despite the fact Rhiannon's looks were something everybody around us constantly felt the need to point out ('She's just so beautiful! She's going places! She's going to be famous! She and Rosie look nothing alike!'), I don't think I realised just how significant the difference was between us until the contest. The child-modelling contest I entered, which Rhiannon proceeded to win.

That was the exact moment I realised I was the Doug Pitt to my sister's Brad.

Nothing can quite prepare you for the trauma that comes with entering a modelling contest, only to have your sister win it. That was the day I figured out that no amount of smarts would ever matter as much as a pretty face. And considering I had been born with the smarts and the average face, I was pissed.

It happened at the 'Some Kids Are Beautiful and Some Kids Are Not' modelling competition at Macquarie Shopping Centre. (Okay, so I can't actually remember what it was called but that title pretty much captures the essence of it.)

I desperately wanted to enter. There was a temporary studio set up in the middle of the mall, and you got to bring two outfits and pretend to be famous for half an hour while a teenage 'casting agent' pretended to know how to use a camera. Then they forced your mum to pay exorbitant amounts of money for photos with a faux-cloud background.

Since I had always assumed I would win an Oscar by the time I was ten (obviously for playing the lead role in one of my many works-in-progress, or Atreyu's girlfriend in the sequel to *The NeverEnding Story*), the kind of star treatment offered by this totally legitimate modelling operation seemed right up my alley.

Naturally, I would be discovered at 'the studio' (literally three cubicle walls and a curtain) and this would get the Hollywood ball rolling. I think for a kid who lived in a housing commission complex also known as 'The Ghetto', it was a pretty standard escapist scenario.

I was *so* excited on the day. I tried to look as close to Mariah Carey à la 'Dreamlover' as I could, and brought my favourite tracksuit for the outfit change (I thought it would show off my 'fun/sporty' side — important for demonstrating range).

I had my precious $90 fee (a birthday present) in a little envelope that I handed over to the lady/photographer/only person who worked there, while my mum and sister waited outside.

'Oh, so it's just Rosie getting photos done today?' the lady/my ticket to Hollywood asked as she stared longingly at Rhiannon's perfect face. My sister had only come because she thought the whole thing was hilarious, and I was a massive dweeb who deserved to be ridiculed (which was almost certainly true). She didn't have any intention of actually being involved, which seemed to disappoint the photographer a great deal.

She kept asking me if my sister had done any modelling, and I had a bad feeling about where the whole thing was headed.

But I persevered, damn it. I was determined to make this woman see what I had to offer. I posed for about eighty-seven photos while sitting on an upside-down bucket (obviously also holding a giant sunflower, because this was the '90s), then I changed into my sporty four-coloured tracksuit, which had a different colour for each of my arms and legs, because I thought it was important to prove I had personal style.

I worked it, hard. I was like my own stage mother, and I could feel a win in my bones.

Then Rhiannon had to go and ruin everything with her *perfection.*

When we came out of the studio, the lady whispered something to my mum, who whispered something to my sister. Rhiannon rolled her eyes, shrugged and followed my ticket to Hollywood back inside.

I may have been young, but I was astute enough to know that I was being looked over, and not very subtly. I barged through the door (again, literally just a curtain) to see Rhiannon standing in the front of the camera, face entirely unimpressed, getting a photo taken. The lady (who was now looking less and less like my ticket to Hollywood), then thanked my mum profusely for *letting* her take a photo of my beautiful older sister. For free. My ninety bucks stayed firmly in the cash register.

A few weeks later, I had all but forgotten my modelling efforts. I was happily playing Nintendo (*Duck Hunt*, for those in the know) when my mum got a phone call. She looked at me, panicked. Then she gestured quietly to Rhiannon that she needed to speak with her in private.

I should have seen it coming.

She had won. My sister had won the modelling competition. From *one* shot of her looking directly into the camera, barely smiling, Rhiannon had won the whole damn thing.

And the bitch didn't even care. I think she was more amused by the fact she had managed to win a contest she hadn't even entered, rather than excited by the fact she had won. She already knew she was beautiful, people told her all the time, so ... big deal, right?

I, on the other hand, was pissed. I cried at the injustice of it. What a waste of a birthday present. I couldn't believe my four-coloured tracksuit hadn't got me over the line. But it was finally clear to me that day: she was Brad, I was Doug. She was Kim, I was Khloe. She was Gisele, I was whatever Gisele's sister is called.

So, a year later, when Jesus decided he wanted to marry her and not me, I was disappointed, but hardly surprised. That's just how life goes for the Dougs and Khloes among us. Your sister ends up with Yeezus, and you end up with a crack-addicted basketballer.

We had never really been religious. I was meant to be baptised Catholic to make my dad's family happy (I think they were worried I would end up in baby-limbo if some idiot in the neighbourhood hadn't vaccinated their kids and I caught something and carked it). But Mum's concern for my eternal soul must have been minimal, because she never quite got around to having my head blessed by a priest who could definitely be trusted around children. So I wandered the earth for my first few years completely unprotected, blissfully unaware that I was essentially a godless devil child.

Then the Mormons came knocking, and everything changed.

Suddenly it became vitally important that our souls be saved. We were subjected to weekly sessions at some place called a 'church', where we were sent to a room with other kids to colour in cartoon pictures of some dude called Noah. His obsessive need for everything to be done in pairs made me gravely concerned for his mental health, but when I helpfully pointed this out I was rudely dismissed and told to concentrate on the love I have for Jesus. That was their answer to everything: 'Think about the love you have for Jesus.'

Meanwhile, Mum was next door with the adults, wearing a floor-length skirt and participating in some kind of intensive singing group. She started carrying around a Bible and highlighting parts of it at random, then proudly showing her newfound highlighting skills to the men who turned up to our house each week on pushbikes.

After spending a few months colouring in and thinking about the love we had for Jesus, everyone started talking about 'Rhiannon's Special Day', in which she was going to become 'even closer' to Jesus. Then my mum took her shopping for a fancy white dress, and I knew what that meant: the bitch had snagged another one. Jesus had fallen in love with my sister.

The wedding day arrived, and Rhiannon was showered with attention. Lots of conservatively dressed adults kept pinching her cheeks and congratulating her. Then they would pat me on the head and say, 'Awww, don't worry. Your time will come.'

Always the fucking bridesmaid.

As someone with a vast knowledge of weddings (based on my time spent watching Disney movies), I considered the ceremony quite unorthodox. The groom was a no-show, for one thing. He sent some random in his place, who stood with Rhiannon in a giant spa bath. Then, once the vows were exchanged, Jesus's proxy dunked Rhiannon's head under water. I couldn't believe what I was seeing – instead of a ring, she got dunked. At this point I realised that maybe I hadn't missed out on that much. If marrying Jesus just meant ruining your pretty new wedding dress in a giant Jesus bath, then I could live without a proposal. Although it did mean that Rhiannon was now spiritually protected, and I was still a godless devil child. But at least my clothes were dry. The grass is always greener I guess.

Things went fine with Jesus for a while. We got dressed up every week and went to the church place. I tried to do what I could for Noah's OCD and my mum kept singing with the grown-ups next door. We all continued to dress very, very sensibly.

But then, in what seemed to have become a familiar pattern with the men Mum brought into our lives, everything ended quite suddenly. We started staying home on weekends. My mum stopped wearing floor-length skirts. And when two clean-cut young gentlemen with Bibles came knocking at the door to see how Mum's highlighting was going, she shut it in their faces. And locked it.

That was when I knew Rhiannon's marriage to Jesus was over.

I never quite understood what had happened. With the benefit of hindsight, I'd say it probably had something to do with the rules about not drinking alcohol and my mum really, really liking wine. Whatever the reason, it was over.

First Scott the Taxi Driver, then John the Navy Man. And now, Jesus. All in and out of our lives like a flash. But giving up Mormonism meant my mum could go and get pissed at the El Rancho again, and that was where her next epic romance – and marriage – would have its humble, white-jeaned beginning.

You will be in rehab several times before you're ten years old.

Rehab is a lot like camp. That's what I tell people whenever they ask, and they often ask because I've been so many times.

The catch, of course, is that I didn't go to rehab as a patient; I went as the daughter of a patient. And rehab only feels like camp when you're a kid without an addiction problem. I'm pretty sure for everyone else, rehab feels a lot less like camp and a lot more like a place where someone is forcing you to deal with your addiction problem.

It surprises people when they hear that kids are allowed to live in rehab with their parents. I suppose it's probably difficult to picture a twitchy heroin addict asking a ten-year-old to pass the salt at dinner. Like when you see that video of the fat Indonesian baby smoking; something about the visual just doesn't seem right.

But it does happen, and after staying in a bunch of centres (all with deceptively lovely sounding names like 'Odyssey

House' or 'Karralika') I always thought the same thing: For kids, rehab is a lot like camp. And it never stops your parents from drinking.

Our journey into rehab didn't start until after Mum had seemingly created the perfect life for us. She'd found the next man who was going to save us, and it was a time when everything should have been falling into place. Instead, thanks to her affinity for a good chilled box of wine, everything started falling out of place very quickly. The man, who was now part of an ever-increasing list, was Joe the Removalist.

Joe was the quintessential Aussie bloke. He worked a tough job, loved having a cold one after work and watched Rugby League on weekends. His goals in life were pretty simple: wife, kids and just enough money to buy a house with a backyard. Oh, and if he was really fortunate, and worked his arse off, he hoped to one day make a sacred pilgrimage to Graceland – the home of his hero and the only man he liked more than Slim Dusty: Elvis Presley.

Even his life choices had been simple; he became a removalist because he loved trucks, and even today, in his late forties, he still gets excited by a shiny sixteen-wheeler. Joe is honestly like the real-life version of Darryl Kerrigan from *The Castle*: simple, lovely and lovable.

Which is why it's kind of unfortunate that my mum happened to him.

Mum met Joe at the El Rancho, the classiest joint in town outside of the Macquarie food court. (Of course, there was always the Black Stump, but a restaurant with steaks that good was the kind of place you only went to for a proposal.) He was twenty-one and had no idea what was about to hit him.

Mum was around six years older than he was, staggeringly beautiful, and had two little daughters, which basically meant he was getting a ready-made family. He couldn't resist.

I loved him. I would go to work with him on weekends, carrying a single lamp to the truck while he and other burly men seemed to pick up refrigerators with one hand. He started coming to our house at Smurf Village, always in his Stubbies and work boots, and would cook us steak and vegies for dinner – tomato sauce the only seasoning. He made life feel normal. Simple. And within just a few months, he and Mum were engaged.

The wedding was a stunning piece of Aussie lower-class perfection. If there was ever an indicator of what our life was going to be like with Joe the Removalist as our patriarch, that wedding was it.

My mum's dress was homemade by a woman who lived on our street, and was designed to look just like the most fashion-forward dress of the time: Lady Di's. It was a glorious white taffeta explosion, with two puff sleeves on her shoulders that could have very easily hidden a massive quantity of Class A drugs. (I have no idea what 'Class A' means, but it feels like nowadays whenever you talk about drugs, you're always meant to say 'Class A'.)

Rhiannon and I, as flower girls, wore dresses that matched Mum's, but in a dusty pink colour that made me feel like I was betraying everything I had so valiantly stood for when I kicked that fairy-diarrhoea monstrosity out of my fourth birthday party. I was forced to wear pearl earrings and flowers in my hair, and there is not one photo from the entire day in which I'm not sulking about looking so ridiculous.

The wedding was held in the local Catholic Church, and Joe's fifteen thousand Catholic siblings attended, along with Mum's adopted parents and brothers. It felt like we were part of a real-life, proper family, doing a real-life, proper family thing.

The reception was in a brightly lit function hall on the side of a busy main road, so the ambience was obviously just gorgeous. All the regular things happened: they cut a cake, had a first dance, Joe pulled a garter off Mum's leg with his teeth, my North Shore grandparents tried to get through it without looking overly horrified. And at the end of the night, Mum and Joe were filmed walking out of the hall and into their lives together, which unfortunately at this location meant heading straight towards a busy intersection.

Because romance.

Mum soon had an 'It's only been six months since the wedding, wink,' baby, whom I immediately hated. After seven years of being the youngest, I found having a newborn in the house a very difficult and unnecessary adjustment. It also was the first time in my life I realised I had very few maternal skills and/ or interests. Rhiannon would fawn over Tayla, feed her, play with her and love her. The one time I was asked to watch her, I got distracted by TV and let her roll off the couch and faceplant on the carpet. I like to think when it comes to TV versus babies, my priorities were in order from a very young age.

Soon we moved out of Smurf Village and into a very fancy private rental, which was pretty much the biggest and most exciting deal in Smurf Village since the day my dad was found almost dead in the bush. You see, people don't just leave Housing Commission. Leaving Houso for a private rental is basically the equivalent of Princess Mary leaving Tasmania to become ruler of Denmark. They practically threw us a ticker-tape parade as we drove out of the compound. We moved to West Ryde, which is literally about five minutes from Smurf Village, but that didn't matter. We might as well have moved to a high-rise in Dubai. We had *gotten out*.

No more 'quick-licks', no more messed-up kids drowning baby rabbits, no more mentally disabled guy trying to tempt us into his house with Kit Kats. We were private renters now, my friend. Living the dream.

But not even the dream could make Mum happy. And just like with every man who came before him, it didn't take long for her to realise that Joe was not going to be an effective medicine.

She and Joe both drank a lot. Her drink of choice was wine, usually in a box. His was beer, usually in a stubby holder. But it didn't make a difference what they drank; after a while, everything just seemed to end in a slurred argument anyway.

Sometimes Rhiannon and I would come home to nobody in the house. Other nights Joe would take off, drunk and furious, then Mum would take off, drunk and furious, and Rhiannon and I would be at home, not drunk, not furious, and wondering what the hell to do with a baby.

For the first time ever, my mum was the one filling my body with toxic butterflies.

And that's when the rehab trips started. First it was shorter trips in smaller halfway houses, and because Rhiannon, Tayla and I were so young, and Mum was 'making a genuine effort' to help herself, we were allowed to live with her whenever she went. But every time the rehab was over and we would come home, she'd head straight to the fridge and fill her glass from a chilled box of wine.

So, the trips started to become longer, and we would stay in larger, more permanent facilities. Rhiannon and I would make friends, start at new schools (trying to explain to the kids what it meant when the principal said to your new teacher, 'We've got another one from the bloody rehab').

I knew the Serenity Prayer by heart and I wasn't even eight years old, and I had started to think that 'accepting the things I cannot change' referred to the fact that rehab would never change anything.

But then came Karralika. The place that would definitely stop Mum going to the fridge and then disappearing for days. The place that would stop her wanting to drink from a chilled box of wine. The place that would definitely change everything. We were told that we were going to live there for months — however long it would take — to get Mum better.

And it was definitely a nice place. Karralika was a rehab centre located in Canberra, which, even though I'd lived in fifty different places since being born, and despite being the capital of my country, was somewhere I'd never actually been. It consisted of a bunch of bungalows that families could live in together, with a massive yard and a volleyball net, and the whole thing was in the middle of pretty luscious bushland, so there would be plenty of places for us to sneak off and play.

Straight away I was dubious that it was going to be different from any other rehab (which by now I considered something my mum just did when she wanted a break). Things were the same at Karralika as they had been at every facility we'd lived at. You wake up in the morning and go to breakfast in a big shared dining hall. Then all the kids get driven to school or day care in a minivan. I had no idea what the adults did while we were out for the day, but I assumed it had something to do with talking about how much they liked wine. After school, the kids would mostly just play together while our parents did more talking about how much they liked the various things they liked that they weren't supposed to like. Then there'd be dinner in the dining hall, after which our parents would have more meetings and we would do homework, which usually just meant watching TV in some rec room. Then, before bed, there'd be 'supper', where you got a biscuit, and Milo and milk in a plastic cup.

Just like camp.

Rhiannon and I always liked being friends with the other kids at rehab, because they were the only kids we ever got to meet whose parents seemed worse than ours. There was a kind of hierarchy among us based on what our mums or dads were in for. Heroin was top of the list, and the most impressive, and wine was the bottom. Trust our mum to be addicted to the lamest thing available. But really, being at the bottom of the addiction list just meant Rhiannon, Tayla and I were pretty much the luckiest kids there.

All the kids felt lucky to be there really, because living in rehab was the only time we ever got to see our parents consistently sober. It was the most stable and unafraid we had ever felt. Living in rehab was the only time I got to make it through entire days without feeling the toxic butterflies.

I felt more of a sense of belonging around those kids than I had around any others. I think because, even though the oldest of us was only twelve (that was Harley – he could put a condom in his nose and make it come out his mouth, and it was the coolest thing I'd ever seen), we all really respected each other. For what we had been through, for what we were going through and for what we all secretly knew we would probably keep going through after we left. I don't think at that age we even knew what 'respect' meant, but there was a sense of solidarity and empathy between us that I don't think can be described as anything else.

And although I'd had my doubts about Karralika being any different from any other place we stayed, there actually was one major development while we were there. It had nothing to do with Mum; she would start drinking the day we left. No, the thing that was different when we went to Karralika was me.

In a turn of events that would shock me and leave Rhiannon completely baffled, in Canberra, I was considered cool. *Cool!* It had nothing to do with me; I was still my usual, clueless, bungling self. But Canberra was like this alternate universe where the cool standards were so low, I was basically like a rock star the minute we crossed the border.

I immediately realised something was up on our first day of school. I was only in Year 4, but I'd been to so many schools by that point, I knew exactly how to play my first day. Things were different for me than they were for Rhiannon. She would just walk into a classroom and the kids would realise they were in the presence of a better human. Not unlike how I imagine it is for Oprah every time she walks into a room. Rhiannon didn't make friends – friends just immediately appeared at her side. By the end of the day, all the girls would be wearing their hair like hers and all the boys would be obsessed. It would take her exactly one day and zero effort to become Queen Bee.

I, on the other hand, had to tackle things very differently. I would walk into a classroom and the kids would realise they were in the presence of an average human. I knew I was going to be low on the ladder, so my best strategy was to try and at least avoid being the very bottom rung. I would generally start with a scan of the room for potential friends. I had to play this carefully – it was a very delicate balancing act. I couldn't go after the total weirdos, but I also had no chance with the cool kids, so I had to try and find the ones who seemed in my league but were also nondescript enough that they didn't get bullied. Sometimes I managed this and sometimes I didn't. At one school I misjudged and headed straight for the cool girls; by the end of the day I was playing the dog in their game of 'house'. At another school I experimented with going it alone, but that was just as much of a mistake. School is like prison – lone drifters are weak and vulnerable to attacks. You need some kind of crew as a buffer.

So, with many lessons from many schools already learned, and having accepted that I would never own a crowd like Rhiannon, I walked into my new Canberra classroom ready to get to work.

What happened next confused and frightened me. I didn't have to make friends — friends immediately appeared by my side. And not the rejects, I'm talking long-blonde hair, probably-all-called-Tiffany cool girls. Everyone kept telling me they liked my hair and my pencil case. There was practically a fistfight when the teacher asked who wanted to be my desk buddy. At recess, I had girls following me around. By lunch, word got out that the coolest and cutest boy in class had an Official Crush on me. In the afternoon, I answered one question correctly and a rumour began to spread that I was some kind of child genius. Waiting to be picked up at the end of the day, I was surrounded by girls wanting to invite me to whatever it was that people did in Canberra. Rhiannon looked perplexed. She'd obviously already taken over her class, but to see me in the same position was a foreign and unsettling experience for both of us.

And that's when I realised what had happened. The standards in Canberra were so low, that I'd somehow stumbled across the one school on earth where I was considered the coolest person in class.

I was a fraudulent Queen Bee.

And I knew we weren't going to be in Canberra forever, so I wasted no time taking advantage of my newfound status. I learned how to control my minions and ruled over the class with a tough, charismatic and fair hand. I like to think I was a good leader, but, even with the dweeb-blinders that my Canberran friends seemed to have been born with, I couldn't hide my true identity forever. I was so far from being a cool kid (my obsession with acrostic poems was proof enough of that), and living outside of my natural habitat started to take its toll. Towards the end of my time there, I could definitely feel the façade slipping away. I was starting to get brief sideways glances whenever I did or said the wrong thing. It was like they were slowly putting a puzzle together, and when the final piece was in place it would reveal a picture of me, wearing a stackhat and riding a tricycle with toilet paper hanging out the back of my pants.

So I was relieved when, after a few months, our time at Karralika was over. Not because we were finally going home, but because I knew if we stayed much longer, my elaborate lie would be discovered. It was an exhausting way to live, but I left while I was still on top, and will hopefully always be remembered by those kids as the mysterious yet impossibly cool girl from Sydney, who swept through their lives like a trendy hurricane for exactly one term in Year 4. (I also learned an important lesson: if you're a school kid who's being bullied and you live in a major city, head to Canberra. They'll treat you like a god.)

Tayla had taken her first steps at Karralika, I had been cool and Mum had completed her twelve steps for the twelfth time. Just another standard stay at rehab.

On our first night back at home, I was still on a high from having accidentally pulled off three months as a fraudulent Queen Bee (although more than a little concerned about going back to the minion end of the food chain). I was excited to be back in my room in our fancy private rental. I was happy to see Joe. Things were good.

Then I caught Mum standing at the fridge, filling up her glass from a chilled box of wine. I started to cry. Not because I hadn't expected it, but because I had hoped there would be at least one day where we could all pretend like this time it had worked. Mum told me it was fine, that I didn't have to worry, that going to rehab meant now she could drink just one glass and then stop. But hours later, the box in the fridge was empty, and I knew that I had always been right: rehab is a lot like camp. And it never stops your parents from drinking.

You will get caught masturbating while watching *Rugrats*.

My mum may have loved wine, and she may have disappeared from time to time when she felt like her kids were unfairly preventing her from drinking wine, but she also had some golden moments where she managed to pull off some spectacular parenting.

One of those moments, perhaps even the top moment, was the way she delicately handled my not-so-delicate habit of humping my mattress until I climaxed.

I was eight years old, and I was obsessed with my clitoris.

I don't remember the first time I figured out how to orgasm. I didn't even know what an orgasm was. All I know is that at some point, I figured out that if I rubbed my fanny hard enough, I could make something 'special' happen down there. So it became known as my special place. I do remember being about five, and getting out of bed in the middle of the night to put undies on so I would have better friction with my mattress, so I know I started young. I'd had my own room at Smurf Village, and with that kind of privacy I managed to squeeze three or four special place sessions in each night. I'm surprised I slept at all.

One night, after a particularly good special place explosion, I lay in my bed, staring thoughtfully out the window, knowing that I had discovered the exact job I wanted when I grew up. I wanted to get paid to have special place explosions all day long. I had no idea if such a job existed, or that my mum had firsthand experience of it, but I couldn't imagine a life where I didn't touch my fanny at least three times a day. (Sidenote: this also set me up for a massive amount of disappointment when I first started having sex. After watching many sex scenes in many movies, and after seventeen years of getting myself off on cue, I was under the assumption that I would have a special place explosion every time a penis entered my vagina. How wrong I was.)

Things had been good at Smurf Village. I'd privately built up a lot of experience and felt that I had my technique down to a fine art. I could get the urge and be done within half an hour. Then Mum married Joe the Removalist and we moved into our fancy private rental, in which I had to share a bedroom with Rhiannon.

This made things particularly difficult for me, since touching my special place was definitely a bedroom activity. If I'd asked for time alone in our room, Rhiannon would have immediately sensed something was up and set about torturing me until I revealed my secret.

I thought about stopping, just giving up cold turkey, but after a few days without a special place explosion, I was just about ready to drop my pants and hump the first leg that walked past me. I realised that if I was going to continue functioning as a useful eight-year-old member of society, I was going to have to come up with a way to make this work. Humping my mattress was priority one.

I was both militant and organised in my approach. It took careful scheduling and a very particular set of working conditions before I was able to narrow down the perfect time to pencil in a standing appointment with my special place.

It couldn't be at night, obviously, because my sister slept on the bottom bunk and the possibility of her thinking I'd been possessed was too high. It had to be in my bed, because the only way I could make it happen was when I face-planted on my mattress. And I needed about half an hour (it was hit and miss, but generally if I worked hard enough for that amount of time I could get positive results).

So, all variables considered, I concluded that the only possible opportunity for some 'me' time was after school, in my room, while I was watching *Rugrats*.

As Rhiannon was now eleven and had continued to widen the cool gap between us with every passing year, we did not often agree on the same television shows. And at 4pm on weekday afternoons, there was a clash in our preferred viewing schedules. She wanted to watch *Degrassi Junior High*, which was on at the same time as my choice, *Rugrats*. I didn't understand *Degrassi*, with all those denim jackets and lockers and velvet scrunchies. All the kids on that show looked like Rhiannon, and she watched it like she knew it was about her people and not mine.

It was perfect. I put up a bit of a fight at first, just to throw her off the scent, but after ten minutes of nagging each other, I kindly offered, out of the goodness of my generous and horny heart, to watch *Rugrats* in the bedroom, so that Rhiannon could watch her show on the good TV.

And so it began. Each day, at 4pm, I would 'watch *Rugrats*' in the bedroom. With the door closed. In my bed. Under the covers.

Never mind that my head faced the opposite direction of the television, and that sometimes I was in such a rush to get things started, I completely forgot to turn it on. But this was my alone time, and it didn't look like I was ever going to get caught, so after a few weeks, I relaxed into a routine. Once I was done, I'd take a breath, wipe my brow and leave the bedroom, sufficiently flushed and ready to join my sister in the living room for *Clarissa Explains It All*.

It was the perfect crime. Until it wasn't.

One afternoon, I skipped into the bedroom for my daily appointment. I closed the door, switched on the TV and swung up onto the top bunk with anticipation. Lying on my stomach? Check. Covers all the way up to my head? Check. Is the coast clear? Ch – wait a second, I was already off and running. Bless my eager little heart.

I'd been going at it for about ten minutes and it was a particularly tough appointment that day, so I was panting and I was sweaty (the mattress also had a pretty aggressive bounce happening).

In my frustration at the lack of progress, I thought it would be best to change positions. Under immense pressure and in a very time-sensitive situation, I decided to shift my body to face the door instead of the wall, which sometimes worked when I wasn't getting results. I didn't want to take my hands off my special place, though, so I would need to turn my whole body around without using my arms. It took me about three almost-flips (it's not easy lifting and turning your entire body when your arms are clamped down on your vagina), but I managed it on the final swing, all without losing my rhythm. And it was just as my face was about to land back down on the bed, my body heaving around like a mental person in a straightjacket, that I locked eyes with my mum and sister, both standing in the doorway, mouths agape.

The mattress slowly came to a halt.

I froze. Like an animal that knows it can't outrun the lion but if it just … keeps … still … the sound of *Rugrats* combined with my slowly diminishing panting was all that filled the room. My mother gave me one final, pitiful look and began to drag my sister away, closing the door behind her. ('But Muuuuum, what's wrong with her? What is she *doing*?')

I'm not even kidding when I say this: I then proceeded to finish what I had started. I was mortified, obviously, but it certainly wasn't worth not getting the special feeling. Nothing was worth that.

When I came out of my room twenty minutes later, I was expecting the worst. To Rhiannon, this had to be heaven. I was officially the massive loser she had always insisted I was. I humped mattresses. I was a freak. There would certainly be some kind of humiliating punishment she had decided I would have to endure for the rest of my natural life. I knew it would at least have something to do with being called 'Mattress Humper' and the story being told at every birthday party I ever threw until I was ninety.

I was equally worried about the reaction from my mum. Was she warming up the car right now, waiting to take me straight to the nearest medical professional to be diagnosed with fanny addiction? Would she take me on *A Current Affair* and beg the nation to help with her middle daughter's embarrassing 'problem'? I could picture it clearly: me, ashamed, huddled next to her on the couch as she cries and blames herself, saying that she should have known. She should have done something the first time she thought my fingers smelled fishy.

I braced myself for the new, shameful life I was about to enter, and walked into the living room.

And … nothing. It was business as usual. Mum was feeding Tayla in her highchair, and Rhiannon was watching TV. Neither of them said anything to me as I came and sat down between them on the couch. I kept waiting for the humiliating bomb to drop, but it never did. To my shock and cautious confusion, Rhiannon kept her mouth shut. She couldn't look me in the eye, but she kept her mouth shut.

Something had happened. Some agreement had been made before I walked into the living room. If you can tell when people have just been talking about you, then you can definitely tell when they've just been talking about you and your vagina.

My mother had somehow negotiated a vow of masturbatory silence, and I don't think I'd ever loved her more than I did in that moment.

The incident was never spoken of again – by her or Rhiannon – and she discreetly made sure I had the bedroom to myself at 4pm on weekdays from that point on.

In fact, aside from warning me to always wipe from front to back and to scrub it properly in the shower, she pretty much left me to my own devices when it came to my special place. She didn't make me feel ashamed and didn't embarrass me with a talk about my 'body'; she just let me figure things out for myself, in a healthy, private way. Which I did. Many, many times. I don't think I actually saw one episode of *Rugrats* that year, but, thanks to Mum, I certainly took care of business.

Your dad will finally die, and you'll be relieved.

When I was eight years old, I came to the sad realisation that I was never going to be one of those incredible kids on the news who manages to call the authorities in a time of crisis. Like those freak hero toddlers who can barely talk but somehow call an ambulance when their mum has an unexpected seizure. (And there's always time pressure, like oil boiling on the stove that would have burned the whole house down if the kid hadn't been so calm and brilliant and skilled with a phone.) There are even miracle *dogs* that have managed to alert the appropriate authorities when their owners are choking on their frozen meals for one.

I was always so impressed by those feel-good, time-filler packages on the news, and assumed that if ever faced with the same kind of 'it's all up to you now' scenario involving an incapacitated adult, I would handle the situation with skill and aplomb.

So it was with a heavy heart that I was forced to accept I was not a freak hero toddler. I wasn't even a miracle dog. Because when I was eight, I saw my grandpa fall over, I was the only person who could help, and I froze.

There is something extremely unsettling about seeing an old person fall over. When a young person falls over it's funny, if not a bit cringe-worthy. But when an old person falls over, it's just sad. It makes even the most well adjusted among us look for some kind of way out. I know for certain, even if they don't admit it, that there are many people on this earth who have suddenly pretended to be extremely interested in their fingernails when an old person stacks it in their vicinity.

But even worse than being an adult trying to handle the social torture that is an old person falling over, is being a kid trying to handle the social torture that is an old person falling over. When you're that young, you still think picking your nose in public is okay so long as you use the proper etiquette – you sure as hell don't know the appropriate action to take when an elderly person does something very sad and embarrassing in front of you.

I had hoped that when faced with a situation that could almost certainly end up with me being a hero on the local news, I would rise to the challenge. Instead, as my grandpa was flailing on the kitchen floor, I panicked and woke up my dad. That decision would result in my grandpa ending up in hospital, and my dad ending up in the morgue.

It was school holidays, so Rhiannon and I had made our usual pilgrimage to Tumut. Other kids went to the Gold Coast; we went to hang out with two drunk guys in a town with no McDonald's.

Even though Dad lived with his father in what was essentially a pub disguised as a house, Mum continued to send us to stay there. It was like being sent to a scotch-soaked prison. We would spend our days watching Dad and Grandpa get uncontrollably drunk, praying they wouldn't suggest going out in public. (The best we could hope for was getting through the week without having to walk down the street with someone who only had a fifty-fifty chance of staying upright.)

Every holiday was essentially a run-out-the-clock situation. I would spend each trip trying to keep my toxic butterflies in check, counting down the days until I could go home and not be on the constant verge of nervous vomit.

Now, because I was stuck in the kid equivalent of *Leaving Las Vegas*, my entire life became consumed by this new toy I had (which I'm ninety-nine percent sure my dad had stolen for me). It was a closed flower, but when you turned a key, it would slowly open and a fairy would rise out of the middle. I had seen it on TV for weeks, and dreamed about being the girl in the ad who says, 'Magical!' and, 'Only you have the key!' I think this dream was more about my desperation to be on TV than it was for the toy, but I wanted the damn flower-thing anyway.

I would spend hours opening and closing it, imagining that I was the fairy – but the fairy was a famous singer and the flower was her stage. I couldn't give a fuck about the magic; I was all about a successful career. I had decided pretty young that whatever I grew up to do, it would a) involve an Oscar and b) earn me enough money to buy a house so that I would never have to move again.

The magic-lockable-flower-fairy-thing had also been a pretty good distraction for the week, which, when hanging out with my dad, was always desperately needed. It was the night before Rhiannon and I were going home, and that toy had successfully stopped me from wanting to nervous–vomit on more than one occasion. When Dad suggested we go fishing after he'd had seventeen drinks, I would just unlock the flower and imagine myself emerging onto a stage, the first ever person to be accepting an Oscar, Grammy, Emmy and Tony on the same night. (It didn't need to make sense, it just needed to involve copious amounts of glory. My dad could barely stand up – a girl needs her escapism.)

So there I was, on our last night in Tumut, sitting on the couch and enjoying picturing myself rising like a phoenix out of the flower, with enough money in my bank account to buy a house that I could live in forever. It was imaginative bliss.

Then Grandpa fell over.

I froze. Rhiannon and Dad had gone to bed, so I was the only one available to deal with this situation, and I was at a loss. My immediate instinct was to give Grandpa his privacy. To me, falling over was on par with shitting yourself in the embarrassment stakes, so I figured he would probably just want me to focus on my toy and pretend like I hadn't seen anything. I was perfectly happy for him to get up, leave the room and have us never speak of the incident again.

But then I realised he couldn't get up, and that meant things were in a whole new league. Surely, as an eight-year-old with a serious escapism complex, the responsibility of helping this old man up off the kitchen floor couldn't fall to me? What would the logistics of my lifting him even involve? I'd heard of mothers who had found the strength to lift cars to save their babies, but my love for Grandpa must have been compromised, because I was feeling no such strength. Then I realised I'd been sitting on my arse for thirty seconds while an old, frail man was struggling to get up off the floor. *What kind of person was I?* 'Do something, Rosie!' I kept saying to myself. 'Help him!'

But my brain had gone into complete meltdown. And I was still sitting on the couch, now contemplating my utter lack of usefulness in a crisis, as well as just generally as a human being, when he started to call out for help.

My grandpa was lying on the floor in the kitchen, he couldn't get up, and he was crying out for help.

This was it. I knew this was the point where I had to move. But having now accepted that I was clearly not the person to offer any kind of assistance in an emergency situation, I did the only other thing I could think of: I woke up my dad.

I had no idea what chain of events I would set in motion. I was a little girl, it was late and my grandpa had fallen over. It was confronting, I was scared, and more than a little disappointed in myself for missing my chance to be a hero on the news. I just did what I thought was right.

Dad woke up and saw me panicked. I explained what had happened, and he was furious. At first I assumed he was furious at me for not handling the situation myself. But then he told me to get into bed and he picked up a cricket bat from the corner of the room. That's when I realised he wasn't angry with me, he was angry with Grandpa.

As he walked out of the room, cricket bat in hand, he told me not to be scared. Rhiannon woke up and started to cry, which seemed to make him even more furious. He said that he was going to fix it, that soon Grandpa wouldn't be scaring us anymore.

I realised immediately, toxic butterflies swarming my entire body, that I had made the wrong decision in getting my dad involved.

But I didn't say anything. I just got into the bed with Rhiannon like I was told, and lay there in silence as Dad walked down the hall with the cricket bat. I lay in there in silence and listened to Grandpa screaming as Dad beat him in the kitchen. I didn't say a word when Rhiannon became hysterical. I didn't say a word when Dad came back to bed and told us that he'd fixed the problem. I didn't ask Dad why he was hurting Grandpa. I didn't ask if he'd helped him get up. I didn't say anything when Dad picked up the cricket bat, and went back to the kitchen, over and over and over again. I just lay there, petrified, in complete silence, as the abuse went on for hours.

And all the way through, Dad kept coming back to the bedroom, acting like our hero. Acting like the cricket bat was his secret weapon, and that it would protect us from harm. Telling us that it was going to be okay, that he wouldn't let Grandpa scare us anymore. The more we cried, the more determined he became to protect us. And the more determined he became, the faster he would disappear from our room with the cricket bat.

Eventually, after hours of Dad going to and from the kitchen, Rhiannon and I realised that the only way to stop the attack was to stop crying, to stop showing that we were afraid, and to pretend that we were asleep. We weren't hero toddlers. We weren't miracle dogs. And that was the only plan we could think of – if Dad couldn't see us crying, maybe he'd stop.

So, as we lay in bed together, holding each other, listening to Grandpa's shrieks of pain as the cricket bat made contact with his body again and again, Rhiannon and I closed our eyes tight, and tried to sleep.

I was shocked when Grandpa joined us for breakfast the next morning. He walked slowly and was covered in bruises.

He winced in pain as he sat down, and my dad looked up and casually said, 'Geez, Dad, those are some nasty bruises. Did you fall out of bed last night?'

Grandpa looked back at him, square in the eyes. 'Yeah, Tony, I did. I fell out of bed.'

Rhiannon and I exchanged a very brief glance, frightened that anything longer would blow the delicate ruse the four of us sitting at the table had decided to accept. Grandpa had fallen out of bed, and now it was the morning, and we were eating breakfast.

I didn't understand why my dad had been so cruel, or why he seemed to truly believe that Grandpa had fallen out of bed. I didn't understand a lot of things about my dad, until years later when my grandpa, by then sober and living a happy and peaceful life, let slip one day that my dad had been diagnosed with juvenile schizophrenia.

He told me that Dad had been an incredibly gifted student. Popular, smart, captain of the debate team, talented writer, topped the state in English more than once, blah, blah, blah. It basically sounded like he was one of those kids you want to punch in the face because they're so good at everything.

But apparently when he moved to Sydney to attend university, something in him snapped. He called his parents one day in a panic from a phone box, naked and wrapped in a bedsheet. They travelled from the country to pick him up, and he was noticeably different. Depressed, withdrawn, changed. A shadow of the former cheeky debate captain who had left for university. They took him to a bunch of doctors and he was diagnosed with juvenile schizophrenia.

But he was never treated. He got the diagnosis and then … nothing. Juvenile schizophrenia explained Dad's breakdown at university, and once they had that explanation, the family moved on.

My grandpa didn't seem to understand why I was so dumbfounded by this information. To him, the schizophrenia was one line in a story that he didn't like to tell. He mentioned it like it was an unessential detail in our history – just something he had been told by a doctor one day.

But to me, it was the only detail that mattered. If accurate, a diagnosis like that explained so much about my dad. It explained why he went from a promising student to a quivering naked mess in a phone box. It explained why he could never hold down a job, and why he started drinking and eventually stopped working completely. It explained the gun and the landlord and the bikies and the drugs. It explained why he filled entire pages of journals believing he was someone else. It explained why sometimes I would pick up the other phone while he was mid-conversation and find him talking to a dial tone.

But most of all, if true, my dad's having schizophrenia would explain the part of him that had always scared me most of all: his cruelty.

He beat my mother constantly, often for bizarre and nonsensical reasons. Once, at the end of dinner at a friend's house, he decided to steal a bunch of eggs from their fridge and hide them in his pockets. Upon finding some of them had broken by the time he got home, he took my mum's head and repeatedly bashed it into a wall. He would hide cockroaches at the bottom of her coffee, or sneak speed into her food and laugh as her mood went into overdrive and she didn't understand why. He would play mind games with Rhiannon and me, seeming to take pleasure in our devastated begging when he would accuse us of not loving him, or tell each of us that we were his favourite and the only daughter he cared about.

If my dad had schizophrenia, it would explain all of that. And it would explain why he had spent hours hitting Grandpa with a cricket bat, just because he had fallen and couldn't get up.

It's much easier to think of your dad as mentally unwell and not just a violent drunk. But I suppose on the night Dad was beating him, it didn't make a difference to Grandpa what diagnosis he'd once been given.

The day after Dad had 'saved' us with the cricket bat, Rhiannon and I went home. We nervously told Mum what had happened the night before, and she was horrified. She called Dad and told him that he was never, ever going to see us again. Grandpa was taken to hospital and Dad was left home alone, forced to face the fact that he had beat his own father, disgusted the woman he loved and terrified his daughters.

When Mum told us we didn't have to go to school one morning a few days later, I knew immediately that Dad was dead. She sat between Rhiannon and me on the couch, put her arms around us, and told us through heaving sobs that Dad had died. He had been found by a friend, sitting in the living room, covered in his own vomit. The phone was off the hook and there was an empty bottle of pills. Grandpa, still in hospital from his beating, had to go down to the morgue to identify the body. They both ended up on different floors of the same hospital, because my grandpa had fallen over and I had been too scared to help him get up.

But Mum didn't tell us any of that. When you're little and someone dies, you're just told that they 'died' and you accept it without asking for further details. So, sitting there on that couch with Mum between us, that's what my older sister and I did.

I didn't know how to react. I looked over at Rhiannon for guidance. She had burst into tears, so I assumed that's what was expected of me. But I felt nothing. I couldn't do it, I just couldn't cry. Mum and Rhiannon were both hysterical, and I just sat there in silence, thinking about how now I would definitely win the costume contest at school, because how could you not give first prize to the kid whose dad had just died?

In fact, I went back to school the next day, and was probably more upset about not winning the costume contest with a dead dad on my side than I was about actually having a dead dad.

Mum has held my lack of emotion during this time against me for years. Whenever she's drunk and feeling overly dramatic, she'll wave a glass of wine in my face and yell, 'You didn't even cry when your own father *died*. Rhiannon couldn't even get out of bed and you went back to school the *next day*.'

And it's true. I was emotionless. After the funeral, I spent the wake doing twirls in the church hall because I liked the way my dress flared out like a flamenco dancer's. Everyone kept telling my mum that I was young and I didn't understand, but they were wrong. I did understand. My dad was dead. And I couldn't cry because all I felt was relief. I would never have to go and stay with him again. He would never give me toxic butterflies again. I would never vomit again when someone told me he was nearby.

I spent a long time trying to force myself into feeling something, by concentrating on the one happy memory I had with my dad. I figured if I could focus on that, I could hopefully squeeze out something resembling tears and ultimately get my mum off my back.

The memory involves a yellow chair.

For a while when I was little, every morning at about 4am, my dad and I would snuggle in a yellow armchair in front of the TV. It was more of a mustard-gold than yellow, but I was five, and when you're five there are literally only seven colours that exist in the world, and to me this chair was yellow.

I'd found him there one morning when I wandered out of bed, and could immediately tell that something was different about him. His eyes didn't seem as glassy, and his breath not as pungent. He scooped me up in his arms and put me on his lap, not struggling at all with his balance. He made me a cheese and tomato sandwich with the crusts cut off, which I ate while we watched *Rage* together. Then I fell asleep, nuzzled into his chest, feeling something warm and comfortable in my body that was completely foreign to me when it came to my dad. It turns out that at 4am, my dad didn't give me the toxic butterflies.

I woke up later in the morning, still on the yellow armchair but now by myself, covered with a blanket. Dad had moved to the kitchen table, and I could tell straight away that our special time was over. He had his coffee mug next to him, which was always filled with scotch, and my stomach turned as the toxic butterflies once again started to flap their wings.

But nothing is more of a sponge than a kid desperate for their parents' love, so every morning from that point on, my body would rouse me at 4am like clockwork, and I would go and sit with my dad on the yellow armchair, soaking up as much of this fleeting version of him as I could get.

Of course, I know now that Dad was up at 4am because he couldn't make it through the night without needing a drink. My body was waking up because it craved him; his was waking up because it craved scotch.

The cravings for the things we loved, however different, just put us together during a magic window in his day. At 4am, he had slept just enough that he'd sobered up a bit from the night before, and if I got out there before his first mug full of scotch kicked in for the day, I could take advantage of the magic window. I could talk to him, laugh with him, and eat a cheese and tomato sandwich with the crusts cut off. All while snuggling in the yellow armchair in front of the TV.

It's a nice memory, and I tried so hard to think about that chair whenever I felt like I didn't feel enough about my dad, like I wasn't upset enough or broken enough.

But that yellow armchair would be the chair that he would die in. I literally had one happy memory of my dad, and he died on it. *He died on it.*

So when I think about going back to school the next day, when I think about doing twirls at his funeral, when I think about the fact I never cried, I just think of the chair.

And I don't feel anything.

Your mum will chase you with a butcher's knife.

I started making 'Rosie's Chicken Soup' (patented, so hands off) not long after my dad died. It's a complex culinary masterpiece I developed for the nights when nobody would come home, and I realised if I wanted dinner I'd have to figure out this whole 'cooking' thing for myself.

In a trend that would follow me into adulthood, I kept things simple. The recipe is as follows: boil water in saucepan. Put pasta into saucepan (any pasta will do; I like spirals, but it's up to you). Put powdered chicken stock into water (no specific amount, but if the water gets gluggy, you've gone too far). Wait for pasta to cook. Pour entire contents of saucepan into bowl. Eat.

It was basically my more sophisticated take on two-minute noodles, which although lovely as a treat, I didn't think were a dignified enough choice for dinner (oh, how times have changed). Rosie's Chicken Soup would be the start of my lifelong journey with preparing food, which now, along with adding water to things, also includes placing various products in the microwave.

But back then, I was still just an eight-year-old cooking novice, waiting for an adult to come home and make me a goddamn steak.

Mum had pretty much lost her mind after Dad died. Although, given we'd already been in and out of rehab numerous times, it could be argued that she was losing it well before he sat in that yellow chair and never woke up. Her bipolar was, at the very least, a rubber band that had been stretched to its limit for a while, and Dad dying was the thing that finally made it snap. Even though she had married Joe the Removalist, had a new baby and we were all living in a fancy private rental in West Ryde, Dad's death broke her.

She started going to the fridge to fill up her glass from a chilled box of wine more and more often. Then the wine in the fridge must have run out, because soon she started leaving the house to fill her glass. And she must have had trouble finding wine elsewhere, because some nights she'd be out looking for so long that we'd wake up in the morning and she still wouldn't be home.

Then the fights began. Fight after fight after fight after fight. She and Joe the Removalist would scream at each other for hours, each getting progressively drunker as time went on. It could be fascinating to watch, actually, as there really is nothing more bizarre than two inebriated people trying to have a coherent and measured argument (especially when they both refuse to put down their respective beverages). Drunk people arguing have no concept of proper debate etiquette, so things like voice volume and spatial awareness are never guaranteed.

This can sometimes make things exciting, like when I was once on a train in my early twenties and two lesbian junkies were having an epic lovers' quarrel in the seat behind me. From what I could gather, one of the ladies had found a series of messages on the other's phone – *sexy* messages. And this particular lady had not been the one to send those messages, so a very interesting debate about the rules of monogamy ensued, in which much slurred speech and tears were thrown about the carriage. I thought about adjudicating, but for the most part they seemed to be handling the discussion in a civilised, if not sleepy, manner.

Then, in an instant, things turned physical. One second I was listening to the cheater explain that she had been drunk when she 'licked that bitch's cunt', and the next, there were two lesbian junkies wrestling on top of me, screaming about which cunts are allowed to be licked and which ones aren't when you're in a committed relationship (I think *'Only mine, you bitch'* ended up being the general consensus).

The fight eventually rolled off me and onto the opposite chair (but not before squashing the cake I had with me – we still ate it later, just sort of cutting around the bum imprints), and then things started to quieten down again. Voices were lowered. Tears were shed. Promises about cunt exclusivity were made. By the time I got off that train, I really felt like I had been on an epic journey of romance with those ladies. Whether they were drunk or high, or both (I suspect both), they managed to cover more spectrums on the emotional scale in twenty minutes than I think the average uptight adult would reach in their entire lifetime. It really was an impressive thing to behold.

But when it's your parents (or at least, your mum and your stepdad), and it's been going on for months, it's not so much exciting as it is exasperating. Watching two people who are meant to be taking care of you trying to explain why they hate each other after having had eleven drinks each … well, it tends to make it difficult to concentrate on the TV.

A few months after Dad died, it became obvious that things with Joe the Removalist were falling apart. I may not have hit double digits yet, but I had watched enough Ricki Lake to have a pretty good understanding of when a marriage was over. And this marriage, the one that had seen us escape Smurf Village and head to a fancy private rental, was teetering on the drunken edge. But what really clinched it, what really put an end to our brief happy family and launched the beginning of Rosie's Chicken Soup, was the night Mum got her hands on a butcher's knife.

It was late. Tayla, just a year old, was asleep in her room. Rhiannon and I, in the trusty bunk beds that frustratingly stopped me from masturbating at will, were meant to be asleep also, but the screaming had been going on for hours, and it did not sound like there would be an end to it soon. On top of that, when Joe the Removalist reached a certain level of drunk, he would start to play old Elvis records at a ridiculous volume. So not only would you be trying to sleep through slurred drunken insults, you'd have to contend with the accompanying soundtrack of 'Love Me Tender'. It's an odd audio combination, and not one I would recommend right before bed.

To Rhiannon and me, it was frustrating more than anything else. When you know exactly how a night is going to pan out (lots of fighting, one or both of them leaving, making ourselves breakfast in the morning, waiting for someone to come home), it gets to the point where you just want it to hurry up and happen already so you can get some sleep. We get it: he's an idiot and you regret ever marrying him. She's a whore and you wish you'd never met. Curse the El Rancho (and its irresistible romantic lighting!) etc etc etc.

As I lay on the top bunk, I imagined storming out to the living room and finishing the argument for them. 'Mum!' I would say, Ninja Turtle pyjamas doing nothing to assert my authority. 'Joe thinks you're a whore, and would like you to kindly get out of his face so he can listen to Elvis in peace. Joe:

Mum hates you and wishes you were dead. She regrets the day she ever met you and thinks your Maseur sandals are ugly. Are we in agreement?'

They would look at me, shocked, but no doubt impressed by my ability to break down all the problems in their marriage so accurately and succinctly.

'Good. Now kindly sign here so we can finalise this divorce and Rhiannon, Tayla and I *can get some damn sleep.*'

I would then march back to bed, legal documents in hand (I'm sure I would figure out what to do with them later), and leave Mum and Joe the Removalist embarrassed that they needed an eight-year-old girl to tell them what should have been glaringly obvious from the moment Elvis first started playing at full blast: the marriage was over.

But that night, I didn't have time to go ahead with my conflict resolution fantasy. Before I had begun to even contemplate whether I would actually do it, I heard Joe scream. A terrified scream. Then I heard Mum laugh, and both of them started running towards our room.

I hung my head over the side of the top bunk and looked down at Rhiannon. Something bad was about to happen. Joe crashed through the door of our room, turned the main light on and closed the door behind him. Then he put his body up against the door and started screaming at us. 'Move the bed!' he was saying. 'Help me!'

Rhiannon and I stood in the middle of the room, unsure what the hell was going on. Just a minute earlier we had been under the covers, listening to the soothing sounds of a drunken argument by nightlight. Now we were standing in a starkly lit room, being ordered to move a bunk bed that to us might as well have weighed eleven tonnes.

Then the knife appeared under the door.

'Joooe … Jooooe! Come out, Joey baby,' my mum chanted, as she tried to stab at his feet with the knife. Rhiannon started screaming. Joe was screaming. He was trying to hold the door closed just as hard as Mum was trying to force her way in. She kept stabbing at the door with the knife, laughing. The silver blade would disappear and then all of a sudden slip through a crack in the side.

'Move the bed to the door. Now!' Joe was hysterical, and he couldn't keep holding the door not knowing where the knife would stick through next. But it was a giant fucking bunk bed, and there's no way Rhiannon and I were going to be able to slide that thing across the room. I had made it my life's mission to get out of PE by pretending I was seriously afraid of the risk of melanoma — there's no way I had the physical stamina required to move a bed. Rhiannon, with her tiny, perfect, delicate little model body was equally as inept.

The only option was for us to go and get help.

Rhiannon leapt into action. If I hadn't had her lead to follow, I would have just stood in the middle of the room, frozen and staring at the knife poking through the door until my mum knocked it down. But Rhiannon went into superhero mode.

'The window,' she said, snapping me out of my trance and pulling me over to it. 'We need to climb out, jump onto the balcony and go next door for help.'

Our bedroom window was two storeys high, with the balcony a couple of metres to the left and about a metre below. We would have to scale the side of the house, jump down onto the balcony and pray we didn't miss. Once there, it connected to the driveway, so we could safely escape and find someone to help Joe.

I looked at Rhiannon, petrified. But the determination on her face told me this was no time to argue, or to point out that she was a notoriously shitty climber. She went first. There were some bricks on the side of the house that stuck out a little further than the others, and she used those to stand on. But there was nothing to hold on to, so she just clung to the blinds from the window as long as she could, before letting go and hugging the side of the house as she made her way across to the balcony. She jumped, and she made it, so I followed. (Yes, I waited to see if she made it before I followed. It's called not being a dummy.)

Once free of the house, we climbed the fence into our neighbours' yard and bashed on the back door as hard as we could.

And that's all I remember. After that, everything goes black, and all I see when I close my eyes is the knife through the door.

I woke up the next morning in my own bed. Rhiannon was asleep on the bunk beneath me. For a second I hoped that I had dozed off while planning Mum and Joe's divorce, and all of it had just been a nightmare. I wandered out to the living room, hoping to see Mum feeding Tayla in her highchair and Joe watching TV. Hoping my mum would make me breakfast and give me a hug and ask me what I wanted to do that day.

But they weren't there. The TV *was* on, and Tayla *was* in her highchair, but she was being fed by a lady I didn't recognise. That didn't faze me so much — growing up with parents who like to drink means you often wake up to random adults taking care of you. These people — family, friends, neighbours — would generally look at you with pity then take you shopping and buy you something. So, while your parents hadn't come home and that was always a slight cause for concern, any bad feelings were generally outweighed by your new Polly Pocket.

The lady feeding Tayla that day said she was an old school friend of my mum's. 'Something happened last night, sweetie. And your mum and dad just needed me to watch you for a while.'

'He's not my dad,' I said, looking in disgust at what she had chosen to give Tayla for breakfast. It was toast with Vegemite and mashed banana. I wasn't thrilled about having a baby in the house, but even I felt sorry for Tayla and the fact that she had

95

zero autonomy over her body and was therefore being forced to eat the tragedy on the plate in front of her.

'Do you want me to make you some breakfast?' the random asked, clearly misinterpreting the look on my face as some kind of desire.

'Um, no.' I said, slowly backing out of the room. I almost considered that breakfast more of a crime than what had occurred the night before.

The butcher's knife incident was, sadly, the end of our time in the fancy private rental. Oh, and also the end of Mum's marriage to Joe the Removalist. Mum, Rhiannon, Tayla and I packed our things and moved back into a Houso house, although we were in a regular neighbourhood this time, rather than a Smurf Village–style ghetto (which meant we at least didn't have to worry about getting pregnant as soon as we hit puberty).

This was when I developed Rosie's Chicken Soup (again – patented, so hands off). It was nice to have the constant fighting over, although I have to admit I did kind of miss the Elvis. But living alone with Mum meant there was no longer a Joe buffer when she took off to find wine, so every time she left we were definitely going to be fending for ourselves.

One night, with Rhiannon at a friend's and Tayla with relatives, it was just me and Mum. Which meant that within about twenty minutes, it was just me. I killed a few hours watching TV, then, realising dinner was on my shoulders, came up with the brilliant concept of Rosie's Chicken Soup. I burned half the pasta to the bottom of the saucepan, but managed to get a fairly enjoyable meal out of it nonetheless (a meal I continue to enjoy to this day, by the way).

It was at about 10pm that I started to get scared. I had seen Stephen King's *It* way too young, which basically guaranteed that any time I was alone I became convinced that a devil clown was going to try and rip my limbs off and eat my heart. I started to panic when it didn't look like Mum was coming home. With Rhiannon, I could handle it. But an entire night *by myself*? Forget it. I had to get out of there and save my limbs while I still had the chance.

This was the era of home phones, and there was only one number I could remember: the number that had recently been mine – Joe the Removalist's house. Joe continued to see us girls after he and Mum divorced, so I assumed the knife incident had been forgiven (at least, my mum wasn't in prison, so I considered that a good sign). I knew Joe would probably be home, and he was a good man, so I knew that if I asked, he would come and save me. I was also sick of the crappy new Houso house, and missed the fancy private rental where I had briefly felt like I was part of a proper family. I wanted to feel the feeling of being in that house again, so I called him.

I should have known as soon as I heard Elvis blaring down the phone that he was drunk. Too drunk to drive, in fact, which meant he couldn't pick me up. But I was used to drunk adults — what I didn't want was to be attacked by a Stephen King character and spend the rest of my life in a wheelchair. There must have been enough panic in my voice to tug at Joe's heartstrings, because he sent a taxi to come and get me.

I packed a little bag with my toothbrush and waited in the front yard — I had never been in a taxi by myself before and had no clue what it would entail, but I was determined to come across as a seasoned traveller. I was debating whether I should sit in the front or the back when the taxi pulled up. The driver seemed … suss. And rightfully so. Here was an eight-year-old, alone, standing in the front yard of a house that clearly had no one inside. I was holding a little backpack, and spent at least three minutes circling the car trying to decide which door to open. Eventually he got out and opened one of the back doors for me.

'Thank you, sir,' I said, in an accent that I hoped would convince him I was a royal who had somehow lost her private car and taken a wrong turn.

I tried to act like it was all the most natural thing in the world and that getting in taxis on my own at 11pm on Saturday night was totally something that I did all the time. I told him the address — still in an accent that sat somewhere between British and delusional — and he started driving.

When I arrived at Joe's place, things were not as I remembered them. He paid the taxi driver, swaying a little as he did so, and took me inside. The house was literally devoid of furniture, which, although ironic for a removalist, made sense, seeing as we had all the furniture at our new house. There wasn't even a TV, and since TV had been my best friend since I could remember, this made me nervous.

I had been hoping to find the warm, family home that had (however briefly) made me feel safe. Instead, I was faced with a drunken removalist, sitting on a milk crate in an empty living room, listing to Elvis records through headphones. He made up some blankets for me on the floor of the bedroom I had shared with Rhiannon just a few months earlier. But it was empty now. And dark. It was even scarier than when Mum had been putting the knife through the door.

I honestly don't know what I had been expecting. I think deep down I had hoped I would walk through the door and then back in time, to when Mum and Joe were newlyweds, we had a new baby and everybody was so excited to be living in a fancy private rental. I lay down on the floor of the room I had once hung posters in, and cried as I tried to fall asleep.

At some point in the night, I woke up and, confused and disoriented, decided to head to Mum and Joe's room to see if they would let me sleep with them. Sometimes, if I was really scared or had a particularly bad nightmare in which IT had eaten one of my legs, I would snuggle in between them early in the morning until it was time to get up.

The house was pitch-black, but I knew the way to their room. I ran my fingers along the wall as I felt my way down the hallway. I reached out to their doorknob and slowly turned it. It was best not to make any noise – you were guaranteed a snuggle if they woke up and you were already in the bed. I opened the door and slowly started to walk across the bedroom. I couldn't see a damn thing with the lights off, but I knew it was only a few steps until I would reach the edge of their bed. I walked in the dark, arms outstretched, and when I felt certain I was close enough, I made a dive for the mattress.

But I hit the floor, hard. There was no mattress there, because there was no bed there. In my sleepiness I had forgotten that this wasn't my home anymore. It was just an empty house that my mum's ex-husband was living in until the lease ran out.

I lay there, on the floor, in the dark, heartbroken. I had reached out for my mum and she wasn't there. All I wanted was to snuggle between them until it was time to get up, and now I was lying on the floor of an empty room. I felt like a ghost in a house that didn't exist anymore.

I stayed there until morning, not even close to falling back asleep. I didn't really know it then, but I was heartbroken because that was the first time in my life I really understood that you can never go home again. And I'd never really had a home to begin with, so what was the point of ever getting up off the floor?

Joe, who had been sleeping on a single mattress in Tayla's old room, woke a little later and drove me home. Mum, feeling more responsible than usual I guess, had come home during the night and panicked to find that I wasn't there. She was waiting for me in the front yard as I climbed out of Joe the Removalist's ute.

She put her arm around me, but it didn't feel like what I had been looking for the night before.

As we walked inside, she turned to me and asked, laughing, 'What the bloody hell were you trying to cook in that saucepan you left on the stove?'

'Rosie's Chicken Soup,' I said flatly, and followed her inside.

Your foster dad will stick his hands down your pants, and you will feel so, so lucky.

It's hard to keep up appearances when your mum hasn't been home in four days. During school holidays, it's fairly easy to hide the embarrassing dysfunction in your life – as long as you don't have to go to class, there's no way you can slip up and reveal that you've only eaten Rosie's Chicken Soup since Sunday.

But once school is in session, covering for your mum's latest wine expedition gets a lot more complicated.

In about Year 4, I was at maybe my seventh or eighth school so far, and naturally I had been a premium dweeb at every one of them (except, of course, for Canberra, the clueless nerd utopia where I had so briefly reigned), and my inherent lack of cool meant I had to be careful about what came out of my mouth at the best of times, let alone when I had left my mum that morning passed out on the living room floor.

But Rhiannon and I had become fairly skilled at putting a

hazy filter on our lives. We were like human Instagram before there was Instagram. Add a little 'Valencia' and nobody will ever know that the picture is seriously flawed.

If Mum didn't get home in time to take care of baby Tayla, Rhiannon would skip school and do the job for her. Although there really wasn't that much of an age difference between us at twelve and nine, it was never really under discussion that I would be the stand-in caretaker. When there were no adults around, we just slipped into our natural roles: me, always so panicked about what other people thought of me, would get dressed and go to school each day like nothing was happening; Rhiannon, who never seemed to give a fuck what anybody thought of her, would take on the mothering job and stay home to look after the baby. It should also be noted that the few times Tayla was left in my care, I either dropped her or forgot to change her nappy, so I suppose you could say there were competency issues there also.

Mum wasn't gone all the time, but her 'overnight holidays' had certainly begun to increase in frequency, and as skilled as you think you are at pretending you have a normal life, at some point, somebody is going to notice that two little girls are living alone in a house with a baby.

It was on one such day, when I had dutifully put on my uniform and walked to school, and Rhiannon had stayed at home with Tayla, that we were finally busted. I'm actually surprised I didn't realise what was going on when I first saw the principal knock on my classroom door. She gestured for my teacher Mrs Blythe to come to the hallway, where they spent a few minutes talking about something that looked very important.

When Mrs Blythe came back inside and started walking towards my desk, I was actually excited. I really wanted it to be about me. Had I won a prize? Was I finally being recognised for being a superstar genius? Had somebody found and been wildly impressed by one of my screenplays in which I marry Benny from *The Sandlot*?

I beamed with pride as it became obvious she was making a beeline for my table. Then I remembered: oh, that's right. I haven't seen my mum in four days and Rhiannon and I don't know how to use the washing machine. What are the chances this is about that, and not about me winning an Oscar for a movie I haven't starred in yet?

'Rosanna,' Mrs Blythe said, a look of pity on her face I had come to recognise as an indication something bad was about to go down. 'Mummy didn't come home last night sweetie, and there are some ladies here who'd like to talk to you.'

She started packing up my things, and I was mortified. The entire class had heard what she'd said. All the effort Rhiannon and I had put into creating the façade of a perfect life was ruined. Would there ever be a day at school I wasn't humiliated? (Hint: no.)

There was an old lady waiting for me in the hall. She took my hand, even though I was way too old for that shit (just another dagger to my eternally daggy heart), and walked me towards the parking lot, where her car was waiting. There was another old lady sitting in the front passenger seat (it was like being arrested by the Golden Girls), and there, in the back, like two criminals who had finally been busted after years on the run, were Rhiannon and Tayla. Rhiannon's head was hanging in shame, and I knew we had finally been caught.

The old ladies were DOCS workers. Someone had dobbed us in.

And apparently there would be no more chances. No more staying in halfway houses or rehab centres with Mum. No more staying with a friend for a few days until things blew over. It was time for us to be officially 'removed from care'. The government Golden Girls were out to ruin our lives. Mum needed to 'get better', and this time, we weren't allowed to stick around for the ride.

We stayed with an uncle for a while. We stayed with our birth grandma for a while. Tayla was separated from us and lived with some of her dad's relatives for a while. But nobody seemed to want to keep us. Whatever test you needed to pass to be a kid that adults wanted around, we were just not passing it. We were told that all three of us might be split up — that three girls together was too much of a commitment for most carers. Mum was apparently doing well; she had been to rehab and was now back working as a nurse, but it would still be a while before the Golden Girls would trust her again, so we desperately needed somewhere to live.

That's when we hit the foster home jackpot.

From the start, everybody kept saying how lucky we were. We were just so lucky that anyone was willing to take on three girls, especially when one of them was a toddler. We were just so lucky that they were a wealthy family from Pennant Hills who lived in a beautiful, big house. We were just so lucky that their son, who went to a very fancy private school, was around the same age as us. We were just so lucky that the foster mum and dad seemed like such lovely people.

We were so, so lucky.

And it actually was pretty incredible. The first night we went to live with our amazing new foster family, it was like being in a movie where everything turns out fine in the end. We dropped our stuff off at their Pennant Hills mansion and drove up to their farm for the weekend. Yeah – they had a house *and* a farm. And this wasn't just any farm, it was like a kid utopia surrounded by bush. There was a tennis court, a tree house, a waterslide and a flying fox. Oh, and just when we thought it couldn't get any more perfect, we found out our new foster parents took care of abandoned joeys. *Baby goddamn kangaroos!* We were in heaven. It was our first night living with the foster family jackpot, and we were so, so lucky.

Then it was time to take a bath.

There was no hot water at our weekend farm paradise, so our new foster dad heated some up on the fire outside, then he took us to the bathroom and poured it into a massive tub. He told us to jump in ... and then he just stood there.

My sister and I looked at each other.

'Come on!' he said. 'Before it gets cold!' And still, he just stood there. This was weird. We weren't sophisticated ladies, but we weren't little kids either. We'd each had a birthday since being taken away from Mum – I was ten, Rhiannon was thirteen, and neither of us wanted to get naked in front of a man we didn't know. But he obviously intended to stay in the bathroom, and everything was just so awesome and there was a tree house and we were just so lucky.

So I took off my clothes and jumped in. I didn't particularly want to, but I remember thinking that maybe that's just how their family did things, so I should just do it. That was always my way – so desperate to be cool, so desperate to be liked, I'd do anything to fit in.

Rhiannon, on the other hand, got as far as her undies and refused to take them off. He tried convincing her several times, but she stood firm. They had an intense staring stand-off until she actually just got into the tub with her undies on. To this day, I vividly remember the look on her face. It was equal parts confusion, desperation and humiliation. I tried to embrace the whole thing, laughing as he sat on the edge of the tub splashing us with water. But Rhiannon stayed quiet.

Later that night, as we sat around the fire outside (a campfire because we were just so lucky!), the dad asked me to come and sit on his lap. As soon as I did, he reached inside my pants and rested his hand directly on my bum. I froze. I had tried to pass off the bath thing as a family quirk but this was definitely wrong. Or was it? *Was it?* I was only a kid. Men don't do stuff like that to kids. He must just be playing around! Maybe they just touch bums in this family?

But as his fingers tickled and squeezed my skin and moved further and further forward, my whole body stiffened. I thought of my grandma, who we'd been living with right before we went to the foster family. She'd told me that if anything went wrong, if anything didn't feel right, to call her straight away. And as I sat there, with this strange man's hand feeling its way around the inside of my pants, I stared into the fire and debated whether or not this constituted the need for a phone call.

It definitely didn't feel right. But we were just so lucky to be there! I didn't want to ruin everything and be split up from my sisters only to find out afterwards that some people just stick their hands down your pants to be nice. So I stayed quiet.

We lived there for almost a year and it continued the whole time. I shared a bath with my little sister from that point on, which he always joined us in the bathroom for. My older sister showered alone, but she wasn't allowed to lock the door, and he always found reasons to be in there – like checking if she needed a towel or bringing her a hot chocolate (because everybody drinks hot chocolate in the shower).

And along with always seeming to miraculously appear whenever we were naked, the hands-down-the-pants thing also kept going. Getting tucked in, sitting on his lap, watching TV, getting a hug: the hands were down the pants. It never felt normal to me, but since his wife must have seen it half the time, I just assumed it was normal to *them*, and that it wasn't my place to say anything. And they were just so nice and we were just so lucky!

Rhiannon and I never talked about it. Not even that first night after the bath. Not even when he would go into her bedroom and close the door just to say goodnight. I kept telling myself that we were kids, and nobody would ever think that way about kids, so I *must* have been misinterpreting it. I must have been.

About a year after returning home, my mum received a phone call. It was the police, and they were investigating claims of sexual abuse made by other girls who had lived with the same foster family. Mum called Rhiannon and I into the living room and asked us if anything strange had ever happened while we there. We looked at each other, and after a moment of tense silence, burst out laughing. I've never been able to explain that reaction. I guess we had both always known that the other one knew, and finally looking each other in the face with mutual understanding was a little overwhelming.

We told my mum everything that night and were formally interviewed by the police a couple of days later. I remember we still tried to tone the whole thing down, though, which in hindsight, I know came from humiliation. There was a sense of not wanting anyone to think we had played a part in something sexual – after all, we hadn't stopped it, so did that mean we were okay with it? Wouldn't it be easier and less embarrassing if we all just acted like nothing fishy had happened? Couldn't we just agree we'd had a lovely time and had been so lucky and there were some uncomfortable moments and let that be it?

It was only as adults that Rhiannon and I were able to deconstruct everything that went on and get angry about it. Particularly since the man in question was, as far as I know, never charged. Many years later, I saw him being celebrated on the cover of a newspaper for his charity work. When I called my sister and told her, she cried in frustration. There were also feelings of guilt in there, as investigators at the time wanted us to testify in court but we were both just too uncomfortable with it. Too young, too confused and too embarrassed.

But sitting there that first night by the fire, not sure how to handle having a grown man's hand down my pants, I had no idea what the next year had in store. I had no idea that his hands were going to be a permanent fixture there. I had no idea that while we were living with the foster family jackpot that made us just so lucky, Mum was working hard to secure her next big shift: a man who not only didn't live in Houso, didn't live in a private rental, but *owned* his own home. Mum spent the time we were away snagging herself a homeowner. She was determined to pull off her Pretty Woman plan.

So, about eighteen months after the government Golden Girls came and embarrassed me in my classroom, about eighteen months after Rhiannon, Tayla and I were taken away in the back of a car like criminals, Mum was finally allowed to come and pick us up from Pennant Hills. Then she drove the car straight onto the Great Western Highway, and headed to our brand-new home in the Blue Mountains. It was time for us to live with Brian the Homeowner.

You will get your first period, and it won't be the only blood you have to deal with that year.

'There was red stuff on Rosie's undies this morning, but you don't want to know about secret women's business.'

That was the moment I knew I had been right about Tayla's birth being a huge mistake. Not only did she ruin my life by taking away my elite status as the youngest and therefore most loved child, but now she had betrayed me by telling everyone on the bus that I wasn't at school because I had started bleeding out of my vagina.

My best friend called me to break the bad news. It was the year 2000, which meant we had only one phone and it was in the kitchen, so I had to process word of Tayla's betrayal while surrounded by family. It took every ounce of strength I had not to lure the little bitch over with the promise of a lolly and then bash her in the side of the head.

'Family' had of course, changed a lot by that point. Mum was on one of the best Pretty Woman streaks of her damn life.

After picking us up from foster care a few years earlier and taking us to live with Brian the Homeowner, she had actually grown and pushed out a whole new human: a girl called Isabella. And although it didn't look like marriage was on the cards for Mum and Brian, having a baby together meant things were definitely serious. (Well, as serious as they could be between a man with a serious pot addiction who had met a woman with a serious alcohol addiction while all of her kids were being cared for by the state. Not exactly a conventional love story, but a love story all the same.)

So now there were four of us. Four girls with three different dads, all born to Lisa. Rhiannon was sixteen, I was thirteen, Tayla was six and Bella was two.

We all lived together with Mum and Brian in the house he owned in the Blue Mountains, which, although falling apart, he *owned*. We lived in a house that we OWNED. On a street with no Houso families! We felt like queens. And the house was positioned at just the right spot on the mountain, so it had a view that stretched all the way to Sydney. I would look down over the lights while doing the dishes some nights (only after complaining for hours that forcing me to do the dishes was a crime on par with genocide) and think about how one day I was going to rule the city – striding around with my Oscar in hand and walking into restaurants where my 'usual table' was ready for me in the back.

Then Brian would come and pour his stinky, dirty bong water into the sink and snap me right back to reality.

Brian was actually great. A massive pot-smoker, yes, but he was the first of Mum's many boyfriends who had made me feel like being smart was a good thing. It didn't matter to him that I wasn't cool or beautiful like Rhiannon, and he respected me for liking books and TV and would let me stay up late to watch *Seinfeld*. I liked him, a lot, but being Mum's Richard Gere of the moment wasn't easy, and I don't think life with Lisa and three ready-made daughters plus their own daughter had been quite what he was expecting.

It can't have taken him long to realise that he couldn't change her. She never stopped drinking and continued to take off at will. In the years since leaving the foster home and going to live with him and Mum, my sisters and I had been taken away and returned a few more times. I spent my first few years of high school wondering which family member I'd be shipped off to live with the next week, just hoping to make it through the weekend without Mum disappearing or getting hammered or attempting suicide for the twenty-ninth time. My friends understood that if I didn't turn up at school for a few days, it probably just meant my mum had gotten really drunk and now I was staying with my uncle in Sydney, or with Brian's family on the Central Coast, or with my grandma in Balmain, or with Whoever in Anyplace. Not knowing where anyone in our family was going to be from one day to the next had pretty much become the norm.

But that was clearly not what Brian had thought he was signing on for when he met a pretty nurse called Lisa, who had 'a bit of a drinking problem' that she was working hard to fix so she could get her daughters back. Now he'd been living with Lisa for four years, and not only did she still drink heavily, but she kept losing her daughters like they were car keys. Not exactly the fairytale he'd had in mind.

He resented her, she resented him, and they fought like nothing I had ever seen before. Our house was constantly filled with the sound of screaming. And the smell of more than a little pot-smoke. That house was literally a giant Dutch oven. I had to have been inadvertently stoned 90 percent of the time. Maybe that's why I thought *Friends* was funny.

It was an incredibly dysfunctional household, and one that I expected to implode at any moment. But I was in Year 9 and had just found out that my little sister had told everyone about my first period. An unstable home that smelled like pot and a bipolar, alcoholic mother were the least of my worries.

The actual 'first gush' had taken place the night before. In my sleep, thank Oprah. Having your first period arrive during the night is like winning the menstrual lottery. I cannot describe the relief I felt when I realised it had happened in the privacy of my bed, and not while I was in the middle of eating a sandwich on the playground. You see, from about the age of nine, girls literally spend every waking hour knowing that at some point soon a massive amount of blood is going to start gushing out of their special place, but they have no idea when, and they have no idea where they'll be. All you know is that a blood explosion is definitely coming, and you have no control over it. It's like having a time bomb on your fanny, and that's a lot of pressure for a young lady.

So, although devastated that I now had to deal with my 'monthly', I was relieved that my undies had at least filled with blood for the first time in private.

I sat on the toilet for about ten minutes, staring at my bloody knickers, not quite sure what to do. I knew what periods were – Mum had done the responsible thing a few years earlier, by sitting Rhiannon and I down on the couch, leaving a book in front of us called *Every Girl* and then promptly leaving the room. It was filled with lots of diagrams of naked bodies and the reproductive system and had been the catalyst for my fear of erupting with blood at any waking moment. Rhiannon and I both acted like we thought the book was hilarious, but would then catch each other reading its pages in earnest when we thought nobody was looking. Mum had done the same thing when pesky questions about where babies come from kept popping up. One day, a horrifying book called *A Baby Is Born* suddenly appeared in the living room. It was filled with graphic photos of hairy heads coming out of vaginas and women screaming in pain. All *A Baby Is Born* really taught me is that a baby is born because a woman must have done something awful in a past life.

Anyway, I knew that I was going to need some kind of adult lady nappy called a 'pad'. I also knew that I didn't have access to a pad, or money to buy pads, so I was going to have to break the news to my mum that I had a) become a woman and b) ruined my mattress.

I took my undies off and headed to her room. 'Mum,' I said, handing her my scrunched-up ball of blood knickers. 'I think I've got that ... *thing*.'

She held the evidence in her hand and smiled. 'Oh! Um, it's okay, darling,' she said, putting her arm around me. 'We'll take care of it. Why don't you have a shower and I'll put these in the wash, okay?'

It was just as I was contemplating how to parlay this turn of events into a day off school, when Tayla, that adorable, rambunctious butterball whom I wanted to kill, came barging into the bedroom. 'Put *what* in the wash? What's that? What's that red stuff? Are they Rosie's undies? Why is there red stuff on Rosie's undies?'

'Don't worry about it, Tayla,' my mum snapped, pushing her out of the room. 'It's secret women's business!'

With that, I took a shower (and stayed in there a while, completely mesmerised by how much blood could be coming out of my body without resulting in immediate death). I was successful in scoring the day off school, so Tayla caught the bus on her own that day. There were some minor humiliations in the next few hours. Mum called Brian on his way home from a night nursing shift and asked him to buy me pads. 'Hey Rosie,' he said, as he threw the packet at me like it was a basketball. 'Heads up!' My mum's boyfriend had just bought me maxi-pads – in bulk. I was truly a woman.

There was no talk of tampons. In fact, I wouldn't figure out how to use those things for at least a few years. But all things considered, the whole event had gone quite well. It had come during the night, I'd had the day off school and my mum said we could have Chinese for dinner.

Then I got the phone call from my best friend.

'So, um …' she said, very hesitantly. 'On the bus today, Tayla kind of told everyone why you were away.'

'Yeah, so? I was just sick, who cares?' I could feel a little panic rising in my chest.

'Yeah. I know you got your period.'

My stomach dropped as low as my blood-soaked vagina. 'What?'

'Well, everyone was asking Tayla where you were, and I think she didn't really understand and she was really just trying to be helpful …'

'What. Did. She. Say?'

'She said: "There was red stuff on Rosie's undies this morning, but you don't want to know about secret women's business."'

'And who did she say it to?'

'Um. Everyone.'

The next day, not only did I have to endure the indignity of walking around in public with an adult nappy in my pants for the first time, I had to deal with every person on the bus asking me how my 'secret women's business' was going. I ultimately didn't take revenge on Tayla; I tried to take the high road by reminding myself that she was only in kindergarten, and knew not what she did. But I did secretly hope that when her time eventually came, she'd be in a very public place. Wearing white pants.

As traumatic as it was to have everybody know about my secret women's business, Tayla's leaking the details of my first leak wasn't the worst blood-related incident I would have to deal with that year. I suppose, given that Mum had chased her last husband around with a butcher's knife, I should have been expecting her relationship with Brian to soon reach some kind of glorious, violent crescendo. Just like Scott the Taxi Driver, John the Navy Man and Joe the Removalist before him, Brian the Homeowner was reaching the end of his turn as Mum's Richard Gere. And their final scene together was going to be memorable.

I got the call on the night of the Sydney Olympics Opening Ceremony. Australia lost its collective mind during that time –

there was not a surface in our country that wasn't covered in some kind of green and yellow paint or a person who didn't have a temporary Southern Cross tattoo. I had never really been a 'sport' person, but I was intrigued enough by my homeland's mass hysteria that I wanted to at least see if we would embarrass ourselves during the games opener. I was personally hoping for some kind of disaster involving a giant inflatable kangaroo, or maybe even the misspelling of 'g'day'.

It was also, if I'm being perfectly honest, just something to do. Although I was a teenager by that point, things hadn't really changed for me when it came to my cool factor, and watching TV at my friend's house with her parents was the best I could hope for on a Friday night.

Rhiannon and I had basically grown into more exaggerated versions of what we had been as kids. She was still effortlessly cool, and I was still the opposite of that. She had turned into a bit of a bad girl, still not giving a fuck what adults thought of her, whereas I entered story-writing competitions and finished my homework three days early just to make sure every adult on earth thought I was perfect. I didn't understand her – adults had been rejecting us our whole lives! Why wouldn't you do everything you could to impress them?

Rhiannon and her friends would dress in tight skirts from Supré and stay out late smoking in the park, while I was at home in my PJs watching Robin Williams stand-up specials on TV and trying to do that Titanic sex-hand thing on my bedroom window. She would listen to Tupac on full blast, and burst out laughing when I would bang on the wall because I was trying to read. When Tupac died, she and her friends all sat around in their marijuana-leaf t-shirts, holding hands and crying. I just rolled my eyes and went back to thinking about how I could get cast on a TV show.

The thing that impressed me most about Rhiannon, though, was that she had boyfriends. In fact, I was fairly certain she was even having s-e-x. I couldn't even work out how to get a tampon into my vagina, let alone a penis. Even the idea of kissing a boy sent me into waves of panic. In about Year 7, I had developed a crush on a boy called Stephen, and I may or may not have practised kissing him on Tayla's Baby Born (a disturbing image, I know, but it just had a more realistic mouth situation going on than my teddy did).

Considering I wasn't one of those cool girls who knew all the words to the talking part at the beginning of that 'Never Ever' song by All Saints, I assumed that me imagining Stephen's face while I made out with my toys was as far as my crush was going to go. But then he gave me a note. Well, technically his friend passed my friend Melissa a note on his behalf and she then passed it to me, but that was just the way things worked in Year 7. It said:

'Dear Roseanna, I like you. Will you go out with me? Stephen.'

First of all, my name doesn't have an 'e' in it, but I considered it a glorious poem on par with Shakespeare nonetheless. I had the chance to begin an epic romance with Stephen that would no doubt involve lots of hand-holding and lips-only kissing. And that made me panic.

I was too embarrassed to admit that I liked him, because I'd only ever practised kissing on toys and had zero idea how to handle a real human face. So when Stephen's friend asked me if I had got the note (while Stephen stood hopefully and painfully to the side), I said that I had but that I had thrown it away. Then I spent years thinking that if I had just gone for it, Stephen and I would have had one of the great romances of our time. Like Britney and Justin. Or Oprah and Gayle.

It was certainly a situation that Rhiannon would have handled with a lot more grace. Or at least a lot more pashing. She just naturally understood certain parts of life that remained a mystery to me.

Back at my exciting night in, the Opening Ceremony had just started when Rhiannon called me at my friend's house. 'Rosie. Something bad has happened! You need to go to the house and make sure Brian doesn't smash the TV.'

'What?' I said. 'The TV? Where are you?'

'I'm at the hospital with Mum. Look, you're at Alesha's, right? Ask her mum to drive you home *right now*. You need to go inside and lock the door and don't let anybody in. I have to go.'

Then she hung up. My brain was still catching up with her first sentence and the conversation was already over. Mum. Hospital. Protect the TV. *Protect the TV?* Mum was in hospital? I had no idea which hospital, so I couldn't call back. I just had to follow the instructions. Go home. Lock door. Protect the TV.

Alesha's mum dropped me off and didn't ask any questions. The fact I constantly smelled like pot meant she understood things were a little different at my house, and was usually kind enough not to pry.

I opened the front door to find an empty house that looked like a crime scene. There was blood everywhere. On the walls. On the carpet. It was like someone had taken a water pistol filled with red paint and shot up everything. Furniture was knocked over. Glass was smashed.

Lock the door. Protect the TV. Lock the door. Protect the TV.

Looking around the blood-soaked living room, I couldn't understand why the TV was a top priority at that point. Something had clearly gone terribly wrong. I was worried that my mum was dead, and there was more blood in my house than I could expect to see in a lifetime of periods – who gave a fuck about the TV? For the first time in years, I started to feel the toxic butterflies take over my body again. I ran to the bathroom, and was about to vomit when I realised the bathroom was the worst of all. There was blood all over the toilet seat. There were puddles of it on the ground. Solid, coagulated bits that looked like grape jelly were stuck on the side of the bath. As with so many times before, I froze. I stood there in silence for a long time. I just didn't know what to do.

I couldn't stop staring at all the blood, so I just started walking round and round the house, trying to imagine scenarios that would explain the massive volume of it. Part of me really hoped that Tayla was getting what she deserved, and not only had her first period come at six years of age, but it had obviously been the most epic period anyone had ever seen. Everyone would come home the next morning, and Tayla would be forced to wear a maxi-maxi-maxi-pad every day for the rest of her life. Then we'd all laugh and laugh that I had ever thought something bad had happened, and Rhiannon would say something about a band I'd never heard of, and I'd say something about a book she'd never heard of and everything would go back to normal.

I sat on the couch for a while, in the empty house covered in blood. I figured 'protecting the TV' meant at least looking at it. But even I, only thirteen and possibly television's biggest fan, couldn't sit and watch a TV when there was blood on the wall behind it. I had my own TV in my room, and I just wanted to go in there and lock the door and watch the Opening Ceremony and pretend like the house was filled with people and not blood. So, I went to the kitchen, made myself a bowl of Rosie's Chicken Soup and took it to my bedroom. Then I locked the door and watched the Opening Ceremony by myself, waiting for someone to come home.

In the morning, Rhiannon finally arrived at the house and told me that during a fight with Brian, Mum had kicked the glass cabinet and cut a tendon in her ankle, which was why blood had sprayed everywhere. It seemed like such an anti-climactic explanation. I had spent the night imagining beheadings and chainsaw accidents, and now I was being told it was just a cut on a foot. I was a little pissed off, to be honest. I had come home to a house covered in blood, locked myself in my room, petrified, and I didn't even get an awesome story out of it? Something like, 'I spent the night alone in a house full of blood because my mum sliced her left boob off after accidentally falling on an axe?' No, I got 'cut foot'.

Apparently I had been instructed to rush home because the relationship was definitely over, and since Mum had paid a lot of money for the TV in the living room, she was worried that Brian would tip it over or something.

I couldn't believe I had spent the night alone in that house because Mum was worried the TV would get smashed.

And what was the point of even owning a massive TV if we had nowhere to go? It was Brian's house. He was Brian the Homeowner. If their relationship was over, then we would be the ones who would have to leave.

Rhiannon, always independent, always so sure of herself, moved out on her own. Brian got custody of Isabella, and I went from having my youngest sister sneak into my bed to snuggle with me every night to not seeing her for another ten years.

Tayla and I stayed with Mum, who, after finally finishing one of her longest shifts so far, would need to find her new Richard Gere. Fast.

Your mum will decide she is a lesbian, and she'll pick her new lover over you.

To this day, I'm not sure if my mum is genuinely bisexual, or if her brief fling with a woman was all about the cash. I suppose that if, out of desperation, you can sell your body to a bald man in Wagga Wagga whose head is covered in coconut oil, then letting a lesbian lick your clit when times are tough would at least be a much more pleasurable walk in the park.

And times *were* tough.

After her split with Brian the Homeowner, Mum, Tayla and I became a kind of Blue Mountains gypsy family, living with whoever would take us in. First stop was with some man Mum quickly started dating, who lived down by the local pool. I don't remember much about him – I want to say his name was George? I doubt my mum even cared, to be honest. There was a roof over our heads, which meant she was doing her job.

At least, there was a roof over *their* heads – Mum could only convince her new boyfriend to let us move in if I didn't actually reside inside the house, so she generously provided me with a second-hand caravan that I could live in out the front. 'It will be fun!' she said. 'Like your own little apartment!'

I had almost come around to the idea, imagining myself hosting lavish TV viewing parties with my friends inside my state-of-the-art motor home, when the reality pulled into the driveway, attached to the back of Mum's dinged-up Nimbus, which in the caravan's presence now looked like a Bentley.

There was no 'little apartment' in sight. This thing was basically a hatchback without a motor. And I don't know whom my mother bought it from, but there's no doubt in my mind the man in question is certainly now in prison for something like letting a dog lick his penis, or being caught watching women in the shower while wearing a ball gown in the bushes. It took me about two days just to clear out all the old porno mags, cigarette butts and empty peanut-butter jars. Sperm must have covered every surface. I'm surprised I didn't get pregnant just by stepping in there.

There was space for a mattress, but it was so tiny I'm not sure even the smallest standard mattress on earth would fit. Where did the weirdos who lived in these tiny caravans get their bizarre tiny mattresses? Was there a store where they all lined up, each hoping to purchase their new bed as quickly as possible, so they could hurry back to the privacy of their sad caravan and keep smothering their bodies with honey and cheese spread?

There were also a few cupboards, a small fold-out table and a sink, which, given I had no water connection, was purely decorative (you really should be concerned about your place in the world when you have a sink that's only decorative). And to top it all off, there was no electricity connection, which meant that after dark, it was just me and my torch. Most nights I would get terrified and go inside by about 9pm, begging Mum and her random boyfriend (again – George? Maybe Trevor?) to let me sleep on the couch. I was scared of being raped and murdered, but mostly I just didn't want to die somewhere that had recently been the scene of a jerk-off session involving peanut butter and a magazine called *Miss Mama Juggs*. I may have been a fourteen-year-old following her bipolar-alcoholic mum around in a caravan, but even I had standards.

Next up came a brief stay with friends Mum had made at the Lawson Pub. I didn't mind the time we spent there, actually, since most of those people lived in and around the main strip of local shops, so whenever Tayla and I were hungry and couldn't find Mum, we'd just walk straight into a store and get fed. I'm not sure if Mum had organised some kind of 'feed my kids' tab system, but Tayla and I took advantage of it regardless. We would sit at the Magic Mountain Café eating free nachos and getting that familiar look of pity from the owner, who seemed to know something about where Mum was that we didn't. But we were so used to getting that look from concerned adults; it didn't bother us in the slightest. We would just order as many free milkshakes as we could while we still had the chance.

After a few weeks of taking advantage of that situation, it seemed like Mum had finally found something a little more stable. An unsuspecting man, who lived a bit farther up the mountain in Wentworth Falls, was looking for a boarder to rent a room. He had three kids at home, and somehow, Mum convinced him to let her and Tayla move in, while I would stay in my jizz-infested caravan out the front.

His son and two daughters were all around Tayla's age, and they became convinced that our mum and their dad were going to fall in love and we'd all end up in some kind of trailer-trash version of *The Brady Bunch*. I had zero interest in being connected to those people via marriage or any other means, and I think, despite the fact she was currently enduring the indignity of sharing a bunk bed with her seven-year-old daughter, neither did Mum. The more her possible Mike Brady made advances on her, the more she backed away. She could have very easily made a smooth transition into that man's bed, but it turns out Wentworth Falls Brady Bunch was not a shift she wanted to take on.

So, feeling closed in, and sick of living like a nomadic gypsy (although she wasn't the one in the fucking caravan), Mum decided it was time for us to rent our own house.

Now, renting your own house is a nice idea in theory. But my mum didn't like to pay for things; she liked other people to pay for things, and house renting is generally something that you're expected to pay for. She, of course, bit off way more than she could chew, and found us the nicest, biggest house we had ever lived in. The sperm caravan was sold. Tayla and I each got our own room. Even Rhiannon decided it was worth coming back and putting up with the drinking and screaming and suicide attempts if it meant she could live in that house.

But a big house and a nice house is also an expensive house, and if we wanted to stay, Mum was going to have to find herself a temporary Richard Gere to foot the bill. Unfortunately, she had pretty much depleted all of the Blue Mountains' resources when it came to men, but my mum is a resourceful woman, and she really, really wanted to stay in that big, nice house.

Enter Pam the Lesbian.

Pam liked to wear vests. Long, baggy vests over plain t-shirts and sensible jeans. She was a lot older than Mum — I'd say about fifty — and her greying hair was styled into one of the most glorious mullets I had ever seen. She didn't wear make-up, and her face was lined from years of doing what I assume all women with mullets do — hold the stop/slow sign at construction sites. Her voice was gravelly from years of smoking, and she drove a 1980s sports car that she proudly called 'The Mean Machine'.

Clearly, my mum had decided that if she was going to be a lesbian, she was going to go all out.

'Um, dude, why is your mum going out with a totally butch lesbo?' a friend asked, after spotting Pam dropping me off at school.

'Excuse me,' I replied indignantly, a little proud of my new status as a child with two mums. 'I believe the term you're looking for is "homosexual lady with a mullet". And I don't know. I think because she's paying our rent.'

And she *was* paying our rent. And buying Mum lots of presents. And buying *me* lots of presents. It looked as though, after so many years of searching for the perfect Richard Gere to go with her Pretty Woman, Mum had found him. And he was a she.

Pam the Lesbian was besotted with Mum. Besotted. I don't think she'd ever been in the vicinity of so much femininity in her life. She would lean over to light Mum's cigarettes, and stare into her eyes as if she were the luckiest woman in the world. Mum would then look around at the beautiful house she wasn't paying for, and think the exact same thing.

But I figured if anyone was lucky in the whole situation, it was me. Pam was like a mulleted ATM, and I could convince her to buy me pretty much anything I wanted. It started off small at first – going into Mum's room early in the morning and asking for lunch money, knowing that the naked lady in bed next to her was so desperate to impress that she would definitely give it to me. I saw a pair of Billabong parachute pants in a shop at Springwood, and Pam had bought them for me within two days. 'Ya like those, don't ya?' she asked, simultaneously beaming with pride and looking to my mum for approval.

'I really do,' I said, playing it up way more than was necessary. 'Mum, Pam is *so* good to us. You really should stay with her forever.' *Ka-ching.*

When my friend and I wanted to catch a train down the mountain to watch a movie at Penrith Plaza, I immediately turned to her and dramatically said, 'Don't worry, I've got this.' Then I whipped out the state-of-the-art Nokia Pam had bought me (it had Snake and everything) and called her. An hour later my friend and I were on our way to Penrith with fifty bucks.

My conscience was starting to ping a little at this point when it came to Pam, but the friend in question was a cool one who I had been trying (and no doubt failing) desperately to impress. We had connected purely by accident – there's no way a girl like Bianca would ever willingly initiate a friendship with someone like me. She had massive boobs and pashed boys, and I didn't even pluck my eyebrows. But we shared a mutual friend, and when word got out that I had no curfew and a mum at home who would let me come and go as I pleased, I think she saw an opportunity to use my house as an alibi. She could come over for a 'video night sleepover', and then we could take off and do whatever.

The problem was, I really did just want to have video night sleepovers. Yes, I had the ability to tell my mum I was going out and not come home for two days, but I was too much of a dweeb to take advantage of it. I just wanted to sit in my room and watch TV and listen to Backstreet Boys CDs. And maybe write the occasional Oscars acceptance speech (a habit I still clung to, despite having grown old enough to understand that I most likely wasn't going to be recognised for writing *Grease 3*). But, as bloody usual, I was hypnotised by cool, and Bianca had it in spades, which meant I would go to some ridiculous lengths to impress her.

Every time she suggested something that confused and/or horrified me, I would just act like I was totally on the same page. She once forced me to go to a house party with the cool group, and I spent the entire night watching TV in the living room by myself, while everyone else was in the backyard drinking from secret goon sacks. I could just never relax around those guys. It was like they spoke a language I didn't understand; I was the clueless foreign exchange student whom nobody wanted to have awkward conversations with.

On our way to Penrith after gouging Pam, Bianca said that we should skip the movie and just 'hang out'. 'Hanging out' at Penrith Plaza basically just meant you sat on the steps outside the shopping centre and tried to look cool, while a bunch of other teenagers were also sitting on the steps trying to look cool.

Sometimes you would get up and do a loop of the main street, and then you would go back to sitting on the steps. That was literally all you would do, all night. Sit on steps. Walk around street. Sit back on steps. Repeat.

I was devastated; I really just wanted to watch a movie, eat some popcorn and go home to bed. Now I knew I'd be hanging around Penrith all night, following Bianca while she talked to random boys. We ended up being approached by a car with two guys in it – much older than us, which Bianca loved. I couldn't even talk to boys my own age, let alone two men in their twenties. I walked in silence while Bianca flirted with them through the car window. I was her mute weirdo friend, and I could definitely tell that both guys were hoping the other one would fall on his sword and hang out with me so someone would get to pash Bianca.

She accepted a ride from them, 'just to drive around', and before I could lecture her on the dangers of getting into a vehicle with people you don't know, we were off. I wanted to wear my seatbelt, but nobody else put theirs on because seatbelts were for losers, so I begrudgingly left my life in the hands of a guy wearing FUBU pants. I was not impressed. I just wanted the 'driving around' to be over so I could stop feeling like the penalty they were accepting in order to have big-boobed Bianca sit in their car. Then it was announced we'd be smoking pot, and although I'd spent the last few years living in a pot den, I'd never actually willingly inhaled so much as a cigarette. I was way out of my league. I wanted to impress Bianca, but driving around with two random guys in Penrith looking for a piece of hose that we could put in a makeshift bong was a little too much for me.

The bong was passed around and I refused, because I was 'still stoned from yesterday'. I was impressed that I was able to come up with such a cool-sounding excuse on the spot. I would still be doing that in my twenties, actually, mostly when I worked at a very hipster JB Hi-Fi store. All the staff who worked in the music section were covered in tattoos and drank green smoothies out of jars and would talk about the bootleg cut of something to do with Bob Dylan something The Kills something. I never understood a word they were saying, but I wanted to fit in, so whenever anybody talked about a band I hadn't heard of I would just say, 'I really like their early stuff.' That line got me out of so many embarrassing conversations. And if, as happened a couple of times, the band had just been discovered and therefore didn't have any early stuff, I would act really smug and say, 'Oh. I thought you were a big fan. They've been putting tracks online for years.' I like to think I'm the reason many tattooed hipsters spent hours on YouTube looking for songs that didn't exist.

Bong avoided, I spent the next half hour sitting in the back of the car with the unlucky guy who had ended up with me, and we patiently waited for Bianca and her new friend to finish mauling each other's faces.

I could have had a revelation at that point. I could have spent the time I had to reflect on how I constantly ended up in situations where I was miserable and/or humiliated. Just like when I shat my pants because I didn't want to miss out on playing with my sister's friends, just like when I let the girl who smelled like cheese lick my fanny, I was once again stuck in a compromising position because I wanted to impress the cool kids.

But it would be years before I'd make that connection. Instead, as I sat there, in the back of a random car with random guys and a random bong (and, to be honest, a girl I didn't even really like that much), I came to the conclusion that I had ended up in that position because I was being punished by the universe. It was divine intervention for treating Pam the Lesbian like an ATM. Someone with that glorious a mullet really deserved a lot more respect.

So, on my way home that night, miraculously safe after getting into a car to smoke pot with two strange men, I decided I was going to start taking my mum's sham lesbian relationship more seriously. And I would definitely stop tricking her lover into buying me things. (Unless there was a new NSYNC CD that I really, really wanted. Obviously.)

But my decision to treat Pam with more respect was pointless. As it turned out, Pam had been planning on getting rid of us kids for a while, and just a few days after I sat in a strange car with strange men in Penrith, I found myself in another strange car. This time with my sisters. And four police officers.

I couldn't believe I had ever felt bad about those Billabong parachute pants.

We should have seen it coming, I suppose. Since dating Pam, Mum had started drinking virtually twenty-four hours a day. Usually, she at least managed to get to her shifts at the nursing home, but since her mulleted girlfriend had arrived, things for Mum had really started to go backwards. If she and Pam weren't out drinking somewhere, they were at home getting wasted while Tayla and I watched TV in the sanctuary of my bedroom. Rhiannon had taken to spending a lot more time at her boyfriend's house. There was that familiar feeling in the air – all of us recognised it – like something was about to reach boiling point. It was the feeling we all got when we knew we were about to be taken away again.

Which is why none of us really expected what happened that final night. We'd never dreamed that Mum would be the one to kick us out.

It was late. Maybe around 11pm. Mum and Pam the Lesbian had been drinking all day. Rhiannon was home, and she must have said something to piss Pam off, because all of a sudden Tayla and I were distracted from our TV-watching by what sounded like a fistfight going on downstairs. I told Tayla to stay put, and when I got to the living room I saw Pam whipping Rhiannon as hard as she could with a telephone cord, while Mum sat by and laughed. I ran over to intervene, and Pam threw a punch in my direction. Now, Rhiannon and I'd had our fair share of fights while growing up, but nothing can prepare you for having a punch swung in your direction. Especially not when a very angry looking lady with a mullet is doing the swinging. I dodged it (not particularly difficult, seeing as she was drunk out of her mind), and Rhiannon and I ran over to Mum and begged her to ask Pam to leave.

'Nah! *Fuck off*,' Pam screamed. 'Youse are the fuckin' ones leavin'!'

Mum was laughing hysterically.

'Tell 'em, Lisa! Tell 'em!' Pam yelled in glee.

'I don't want you here anymore,' Mum said. 'Any of you.'

'Mum,' Rhiannon said. 'You're just drunk. You can't make us leave. We're your kids.'

'You're uncontrollable!' Mum screamed dramatically. 'I don't know what to do with you anymore! *I'm calling the police!*'

Now it was Pam who was laughing hysterically. Rhiannon and I looked at each other, exhausted, as Mum spoke to Triple Zero and told them she needed someone to come and take her 'unruly, uncontrollable' kids away. They said they would send a paddy wagon.

Rhiannon told me to go back upstairs and pack a bag for Tayla and me. When I walked back into my room, Tayla was sitting on my bed, wide awake, crying.

'Are we leaving Mummy again?' she asked me.

'We'll probably just stay somewhere else for a few days. Maybe Uncle Ben's house,' I said, as I put some clothes in a bag. Tayla had spent more time living away from Mum than with her. She understood the drill. I took her to her room and let her pick some things to put in the bag. Then we went and sat on my bed, and quietly watched TV while we waited for the police to arrive.

About half an hour later, Rhiannon walked into the bedroom with two officers. They must have been surprised to see that the 'uncontrollable' children they were there to pick up were all waiting patiently and quietly with packed bags. Technically, the uncontrollable ones were downstairs, alternating between pashing, drinking and yelling obscenities about how awful we were. The officers gave us that sad look we had seen grown-ups give us so many times, and told us they would take us to the station to work something out.

Mum didn't even say goodbye to us when we left. The last thing I remember as we walked out the front door was hearing Pam the Lesbian yell, 'Fuck off!' while Mum erupted into fits of laughter.

On the way to the station, I let Tayla nuzzle her head into my shoulder as I thought about all the times Mum had just been a 'mum'. I thought about how she used to leave little presents on our beds for us to find after school. I thought about how she called us 'sweet pea' and 'darling' and would make us amazing cakes on our birthdays. I thought about the time she gave me a special book as a surprise and wrote 'Darling Rosanna' in the front, and how I still considered it the most precious thing I owned. I thought about how she used to stroke my hair when I was sick and the way she taught me to tie my shoes. I thought about how nothing felt as warm or as safe as a hug from her. I looked down at Tayla and thought about how, no matter what, Mum would always be the only person who felt like home to any of us, and how torturous it was to know that the feeling was never around for long. That for each special memory, for each special hug, there were just as many sad and lonely moments when she hadn't come through. She was our only home, and we never knew if she was going to be there. And we were all just so tired.

As soon as Pam's money ran out, Mum decided she was no longer a lesbian and wanted us back. But it was too late. After that night, none of us would ever live with Mum again. Rhiannon moved back in with her boyfriend in Lawson, and would go on to work her arse off as a single mother of two kids. Isabella had already disappeared with her dad, and wouldn't come back into our lives until she was a teenager. Tayla and I stayed with our wealthy uncle for a few days, during which time he decided to keep me and not her. I was sent to a fancy boarding school, and Tayla was left to fend for herself in the foster system. She would languish there until, at sixteen, she was old enough to strike out on her own. I've never forgiven myself for not insisting that we stay together. She was so little, and so alone. But my mum's brother was a successful doctor, and he wanted to spend a lot of money on my education. He thought I was special, and I found that intoxicating.

You will try to fit in at a very exclusive private boarding school (and fail spectacularly).

Penis fantasies. When I was at the College, I started having a lot of penis fantasies. I thought about penises all the freaking time. I was a teen possessed, but with only two penises in particular – the (no doubt tiny) dicks of my bullies, Wayne and Keith. In a strange place and with no way to stop these two boys from torturing me, I began to have elaborate fantasies about horrible accidents in which their dicks would be destroyed. If you'd caught me daydreaming in class during that time, with a faraway look in my eyes and a peaceful smile on my face, it was probably because I was imagining the sounds of Wayne's screams after a blender fell on his peen and switched on. I often thought about Keith getting dick leprosy, and having crusty bits of his foreskin fall to the floor through his pants while onstage in front of the whole school. It may sound extreme ('may'? Hahahaha), but I spent three years being verbally hunted by those boys, and picturing the demise of their (again, no doubt tiny) dicks was often the only thing that got me through the day. That was life at one of the 'best schools in the country'. That was the College.

I should have known I was out of place the minute I was inundated with a sea of pastel polo shirts. Polo shirts, high ponytails and rugby jerseys. It was like stepping into a photo shoot for a yacht catalogue, except I was the waitress serving the models coffee and I kept accidentally getting in the shot. I had very little idea what going to a private school actually involved (besides rich kids and fancy blazers), and when I first arrived at the College, I was still convinced it was going to change my life. I had no idea that I'd leave so broken, that I'd try to kill myself within just a few months. That those damn polo shirts would defeat me in the end.

After escaping the clutches of the crazy lesbian (which I suppose could describe my mum or her girlfriend at that stage), I was sent to live with my uncle Ben, who enrolled me in boarding school within a few weeks. I get that most people would consider that to be some kind of punishment, but I was over the damn moon. I had always been the 'smart one', the one 'going places', the one 'who spent time transcribing sitcoms instead of going to parties', and I felt like I was finally being recognised for it. I may not have ever been as cool as my sister (or ninety-five percent of kids my age) but at least now I was getting a fancy school for my fancy brain. And, given I was about to enter Year 10, I also couldn't believe that for the first time in my life, I was going to spend the next three years living in one place. I wouldn't have to move house depending on Mum's boyfriends, or stay in sperm-coated caravans or throw all my stuff into boxes in under an hour – I was staying put for three whole years. And at a very snooty school on Sydney's affluent North Shore, no less. The freckle-faced dweeb from Smurf Village had *made it, bitches.*

I was sure I was going to become best friends with some blueblood girl called Bitsy Carrington Hastings III, who was related to the Kennedys and spent her summers sailing and her winters skiing. Her family would consider me a Dickensian novelty, and eventually I would become their ward, marry Bitsy's brother and wear boat shoes and polo shirts forever and ever. I basically thought boarding school was going to be like living in a movie version of a Kennedy family photo.

And parts of it were not far off. I was floored when I first saw the campus. I may have been to about seventeen schools by this point, but they had all been of the public or 'public-with-Jesus' variety, so I had no clue that private schools like the College actually existed outside of TV.

There's no delicate way to put this: the College was fucking insane. The campus was so big it was filled with streets that had actual street names. There was an aquatic centre. A TV studio. Two theatres. An amphitheatre. An art centre and art gallery, with fully equipped photographic studio. About ten different sporting ovals that I didn't really understand the difference between. A music centre. A massive gym. Computer labs with Macs as far as the eye could see. A library with fancy electric doors and elevators because it had *three freaking levels*. At my previous high school, there was one computer in the library connected to dial-up internet, and if you were lucky enough to book it for a twenty-minute slot, that was never enough time to download even three-quarters of that picture of the Backstreet Boys you wanted. You would just sit there, watching the image come in, bar by torturous bar, and just as it was about to reveal Nick Carter's glorious face, a scary kid from Penrith would tell you to get the fuck up because it was her turn.

When my uncle took me shopping for my uniform (at a special store on campus that sold only the uniform, because that's a thing at rich schools, apparently), everything I needed just to get dressed every day cost $2000. I nearly fell over. I was fairly certain that $2000 was more than my mum had paid for my entire education up until that point.

I had literally come from a school where some classrooms didn't have enough chairs, to a school that had an aquatic centre and TV studio. I was in an alternate universe, the fabric of which was money and blazers.

The College had boarders and day students, so the boarding houses were tucked away in their own area. Girls were accepted to the school only from Year 10 onwards, so we had one boarding house, while the boys, in years 7–12, had about three or four. There was a huge dining hall where we all had meals together, and I remember thinking on the first night that it kind of reminded me of being in rehab, but that I should probably keep that little tidbit to myself. There were common areas where we could watch TV and hang out, not to mention the ridiculous grounds that were pretty much ours to roam.

I loved it. I was in actual heaven. I'd never experienced so much consistency in my entire life. I thrived on the routine and loved that I always knew dinner was going to be at 5.30 and bedtime at 10pm. I loved that someone came and knocked on my door and woke me up at 7.15 every day. I loved that I had classes to go to and places to be and everything was organised and nothing ever felt uncertain.

For about two weeks, I was so, so happy. I even started begging my uncle to buy me a polo shirt.

Then the bullying started.

As it turns out, the College was filled with a lot of very nice facilities, but it wasn't filled with a lot of very nice kids. In fact, of all the schools I had attended in my life, the College – although supposedly the best of the best – was the only one filled with kids who were outright cruel to me, just for the sake of it. I had never really worried about starting over somewhere new before – I had been forced to be a chameleon my entire life, adapting to different situations and people and friends as they came my way. But nothing could have prepared me for that preppy hell on the North Shore.

It was just so different from anything I had ever experienced, and I couldn't work out how to adapt. My hair was wrong. My clothes were tacky. I used a $3 Lip Smacker while the other girls were smothering their lips in $40 Lancôme Juicy Tubes. I used Impulse while they sprayed their bodies with Chanel. I had never been the cool girl, but I had always been able to at least find a place to slot into, a little corner where nobody would bother me. But at the College, it was like everywhere and everyone were out of my league. I couldn't even find a blueblood girl called Bitsy to be my friend.

I was just too different, and it paralysed me. I was so shy that I could barely talk to some people. And I really struggled with the boys – since growing older, I'd never been friends with any boys, never had any brothers, and now I was living across a very manicured lawn from about seventy-five guys. That, combined with the fact that everything I knew about fashion and hair and pop culture and just being a teenager was apparently wrong, meant that I had no freaking idea how to behave.

I was a petrified former Houso kid, and like a group of very well dressed sharks, the private-school kids could smell my fear from a mile away.

Once the taunts began, they escalated pretty quickly. Keith and Wayne took charge of the mission to break me, and they're the reason I cried myself to sleep for three years, where I would then dream about them losing their penises in a myriad of sickening and disturbing ways.

They were both boarders, and both jocks. They played rugby and cricket, which at North Shore private schools are basically considered religions. The boys who are good at them are treated like gods, and Keith and Wayne had decided I would be their sacrifice.

It was Keith who kicked things off, and to be honest, I was a little confused when it happened. I had never really been bullied before, and it took me a minute to process what was going on. I was walking across a courtyard, when all of a sudden I heard a boy's voice yell, 'Yuck!' from one of the surrounding windows. I looked around, confused, thinking that surely that ridiculously intelligent barb wasn't aimed at me. But there was no one else around, and the yeller can't have been expressing his distaste at the courtyard, since it was filled with the kind of gorgeous gardens that can only come from charging fifty grand a year per kid. I kept walking, slightly perplexed and just wanting to get the hell out of there. Then, just in case I hadn't got the message, the vocal assassin took aim again: 'Hey Rosie! Yuck. *Scabface.*' Ah. Scabface. That one was definitely aimed at me. I had started getting acne not long before I started at the College (a cruel gift from the universe, since my freckles had finally faded and I was actually growing into my looks). A group of boys erupted into laughter, and I looked up to see Keith staring down at me with the satisfied smile of someone who had just hit the bull's eye of a target.

I was hunted from that point on. No matter where I went, there was always a vocal assassin waiting in the wings. And their ammunition never really changed. It was always 'yuck' or 'Scabface' or the particularly well thought out 'Rosie's gross'.

When Keith, who had proudly taken the lead in shaping my misery up until that point, left the boarding house to become a day boy, he passed the baton to Wayne. I always wondered whether there was an official change-over ceremony. Was I bequeathed to Wayne like a gift? Did Keith, sad to think that he was leaving his opportunity to torture behind, decide that he couldn't let it go to waste? I'd say it probably had more to do with the fact that Keith was a sporting hero and Wayne wanted to follow his lead by impressing him. I had a kitten once who used to kill mice and then line them up proudly next to my bed, desperate for my approval, and I think in my bullying situation, Wayne was the kitten and Keith his owner. Oh, and they both had deformed ball sacks.

The problem with Wayne was he had an actual, sadistic mean streak. Keith was just a sports bogan who had hunted me as a hobby, for laughs. With Wayne, it seemed to go deeper than that. He came after me with a vengeance, and seemed to take real pleasure in hurting me. And all the boys followed his lead, either by participating or being too scared to talk to me, lest they also become a target. The vocal assassinations continued. I'd be laughed at as I walked by. I'd be taunted in the dining hall, on the way to class, in the library. I'd be playing sport, and he would come and watch on the sidelines just so he could yell things at me. I started to become incredibly socially anxious. I was scared to walk to class. I was scared to walk to the shops. I was always convinced Wayne or one of his minions would be just around the next corner. I was being hunted, and it was making me a shell of a person. It was exhausting.

I became one of those weird kids who pretend to be sick all the time so they can go to the nurse. And of course, at the College, 'going to the nurse' meant going to a fully equipped six-bed clinic with television, a private bathroom and a cupboard filled with drugs. I quickly figured out where the vitamin C was, and used that as my excuse to visit, usually at recess or lunch when I was too scared to go outside. I invented all kinds of ailments that could only be cured with that little orange-flavoured tablet. Sister Jones, the nurse, took pity on me and often let me use the clinic as a sanctuary, but I hated that I needed a sanctuary in the place that was meant to *be* my sanctuary in the first place.

I started to complain about Wayne from pretty early on. The College was very proud of its 'no-tolerance' stance on bullying, and had very patronising 'No Put-Downs' signs hanging in every classroom. I figured if I said something, Wayne would be punished and the bullying would stop.

The first time I went to the boys' boarding master and told him what was going on, he just laughed and said, 'Oh mate, he probably just has a crush on you.' I must have stared back at him with a look that sat somewhere between 'Are you fucking serious?' and 'Please step back before I punch your face', because he promised that he would 'look into it'.

A few days later, someone had taken the 'No Put-Downs' sign in one of the boarders' classrooms and written 'Except Scabface' underneath it. I went back to the boys' boarding master, who said I couldn't prove that it was about me, and if it was, again, 'Wayne is a nice boy who probably just has a crush on you. Have you tried talking to him? Maybe he just doesn't know you well enough because you haven't talked to him very much.'

I was basically being told that Wayne was bullying me because 1) he had a crush on me or 2) I was shy and hadn't talked to him enough. Either way, the onus was on me to change my behaviour to make him stop bullying me, rather than on him to just *stop fucking bullying me*.

I was furious, and it lit enough of a fire in my belly that I decided I would not put up with how I was being treated. I was determined not to let Wayne get away with what he was doing to me (I also continued to fantasise about horrible Wayne-related penis accidents). I started to complain every time Wayne or one of his hunting party did something to me, however small.

If the College maintained they had a no-tolerance bullying policy, I wanted to put that to the test. But again and again, I was ignored. Told he was just a hormonal boy. Told I should just try to have fun with the joke. Told to accept that it was just his sense of humour. Told to try and open up around him a bit more. He just never seemed to get punished. At one point, when his parents were at the school for parent–teacher interviews, the boys' boarding master told me he'd had 'a chat' to them about Wayne's behaviour. 'They were very cranky, Rosie,' he said. 'Things should be fine now.' I couldn't believe he'd just used the words 'very cranky'. If I had a son and his teacher told me the kinds of things Wayne had been doing, the words I'd use would be 'fucking ashamed'. When I was told they were 'very cranky', I immediately knew that they had no idea how bad things were.

After that conversation, obviously, things got worse. Nothing fuels a bully more than getting dobbed on but not actually being held accountable. The more I reacted, the worse things got, and I refused to accept the notion that my trying to force the school to punish him was just making things worse. I was constantly told not to 'provoke' him by going to teachers about his behaviour, but I just couldn't accept that I was provoking him into being an arsehole by trying to protect myself. He was an arsehole because he was an arsehole.

I successfully lobbied to keep the boys out of the common area in the girls' boarding house, just so there could be one place on campus where I could be sure I wouldn't have to face him. Given I was already of very fragile social standing, my changing the rules so that a bunch of hormonal teens couldn't watch TV together was hardly a smart idea, but I just wanted to be able to walk into one room and not worry about being abused or laughed at on the other side of the door. But time and time again, I would walk into the common area to find him sitting there, often with the teacher in charge talking and laughing with him.

I felt like I was losing my mind. This boy was torturing me on a daily basis and I wasn't quiet about it. I reported him, I talked to teachers, I stood my ground. And still, nothing was done. I was just treated like I was being a spoilsport, and Wayne continued to laugh in the face of the College's 'no tolerance' bullying policy. It's amazing what a boy who's good with a football can get away with.

But then came a ray of hope.

The school counsellor, whom I started visiting just to get out of class, said that he was going to give Wayne an official warning. This meant anything he did after the warning would need to be met with official punishment. There wouldn't be any more of these 'chats' with teachers; something real was actually going to be done. I was so relieved that someone was finally listening to me. I was at the end of my second year at the College, and someone finally seemed to agree that I didn't deserve to be harassed on a daily basis. Maybe, I thought, if Wayne gets expelled, Year 12 will end up being okay.

I decided to wait for Wayne to do something particularly shitty before I reported it to the counsellor. I wanted to make sure that whatever he got in trouble for after his official warning, it was going to be worth it.

It only took two weeks for him to do something at the spectacular level of cruelty that I had been waiting for. And it was probably, up until that point, one of the most humiliating moments of my life (obviously not including the worrying amount of pants-shitting I had done as a child).

It happened while I was onstage, performing in a College production of *Lord of the Flies*. I was the student director, and had been tasked with playing the very minor role of the officer who turns up on the island in the last thirty seconds and finds the boys have turned feral. I hadn't really wanted to play the role, but we needed someone and there were only about five lines of dialogue.

By the end of the play, the young characters in *Lord of the Flies* have become obsessed with the idea that there is a scary beast on the island trying to eat them all, so when they hear the officer rummaging through the bushes, they mistake it for the monster and start yelling, 'The beast! The beast!' Then the officer comes onstage, they realise it's an adult person and they all get in big shit for killing each other and losing their shoes. I mainly just had to look horrified and shocked at finding a bunch of shoeless kids about to kill each other (not a huge stretch for me, given my time at Smurf Village).

Since the College was the College, of course the play was set on a massive outdoor sound stage, complete with a huge, actual plane wreckage that we bought from a junkyard (because 'What's a budget?'). I had a great time doing that play. The cast was only boys in years 7–9, and I liked that I didn't have to worry about being bullied by them. They were just sweet, nice kids who thought I was a drama genius, and it was simple and nobody bothered me. We decided that I would dramatically walk down through the audience, and as all the boys pointed in my direction, screaming and terrified that I was the beast, I would step through lots of dramatic fog onto the stage and reveal myself to be a kick-ass female astronaut. I had a NASA jumpsuit and everything.

The show was great for the first two nights. The audience sat on a grassy hill watching the action unfold, and it was so incredible to see all the kids get that buzz that only comes from performing onstage. I was on a high for those first two days, finally feeling like I had something at the College that made me forget about Wayne. But on the third night, the night all the boarders came to watch, Wayne decided he would remind me he was there.

Everything went as it had the first two nights. I came down through the audience and began to emerge through a thick haze of fog onto the stage. The boys did their usual yelling that the beast was coming to get them. 'The beast! The beast!' they yelled, as I got closer to them. Then, as I stepped out of the fog and into the spotlight on the sound stage, the usual hush came over the crowd. It's a big moment – when the boys realise that an adult has finally found them. There are a few seconds of silence to let the whole thing sink in. It was my job to break the silence; to look at the boys in horror and demand to know why they're all running around in no clothes with a pig's head. And just as I was about to open my mouth to say my first line, Wayne beat me to it.

'Yuck,' he yelled. 'It *is* a beast!'

He and his hunting party, sitting somewhere in the darkness of the audience, erupted into laughter. The vocal assassin had just taken a shot at me, and two hundred people had seen him successfully hit his target. I stood onstage, under the spotlight, frozen in humiliation. I locked eyes with the young actor standing across from me; he looked horrified. I stood there for what felt like an eternity, the eyes of two hundred people feeling sorry for me burning into my face. Eventually, I managed to blurt out my few lines and rush offstage. I came back out for the curtain call, and could hear the word 'beast' being chanted from Wayne's direction along with the crowd's applause.

It wasn't until I finally made it back to my room that night that I could let the full effect of the assassin's shot take hold. I collapsed onto the ground and had what I only realised years later was my first panic attack. I could only manage to get up off the floor when my despair and humiliation turned to rage. How fucking *dare* he? Then my rage turned to elation. This was it – considering he'd been given an official warning, this was the thing that was going to get him kicked out. I may have just been laughed at while literally standing under a spotlight in front of a crowd of people, but it would be worth it if it meant I could spend my last year at this school not feeling like I was being hunted every day.

I went into action mode. I knew all the boarders had been in the audience that night, so I told the teacher on duty in the boys' boarding house what had happened. 'That doesn't sound like Wayne,' he said, incredulous.

'Everybody was there,' I said, defiant. 'Everybody heard it. Ask them.'

So he did. One by one, boarders were pulled into the teacher's office and asked whether Wayne had yelled that I was a beast and burst into hysterical laughter while I was standing onstage in the middle of performing a play. And one by one, they all denied having heard anything. Or, if they admitted to hearing something, they said they couldn't be sure who had said it. I had expected denials from his hunting buddies, but not from the few people I considered my friends. I went to bed devastated, but not without hope. I still had the secret deal I'd arranged with the counsellor. Wayne had been given an official warning about making my life a daily torture, and now he had fucked up. I fell asleep confident that as of the next day, Wayne would be gone, and I'd be free. And I was still holding out hope for that penis accident.

When I reported it to the counsellor the next morning, he said, 'Oh, um, I haven't actually managed to catch up with Wayne yet.'

I stared at him in disbelief. 'What?' I said, tears welling up in my eyes. 'What do you mean? You were meant to have done it over two weeks ago. You promised you would be giving him a warning.'

'I know, I'm sorry, I just haven't really had a chance to talk to him yet.'

'*What the fuck does that mean?*' I yelled. 'You're a fucking teacher! You don't just wait until you bump into him in the fucking hall. You have him brought to your office and you talk to him whenever you fucking want!'

The counsellor just sat in silence, the look on his face making it obvious he thought I was deranged. And that's probably because I was. I was having relentless fucking fantasies about dicks in blenders, for fuck's sake. I was losing it. And I thought that it had all been going to end that day.

Instead, without the promised 'official warning', and with no students willing to admit they'd seen him do it, the whole thing was put down to another 'boys will be boys' incident. Apparently, it 'just sounded like someone was trying to be funny', and maybe I should 'just laugh it off'.

I was defeated. I was done. From that day, I disappeared into a hole. The social anxiety turned into depression, which turned into suicidal thoughts. The toxic butterflies from my childhood came back, and sat in the pit of my stomach like a poison I couldn't get rid of. I started skipping class, stopped studying, never handed in homework. I was in detention more often than not. My uncle was becoming increasingly frustrated with my abysmal report cards. I was wasting his money, and he was pissed off, but I was too embarrassed to tell him the extent of how bad things were. I was stuck in a preppy nightmare, and I hadn't even met one damn person named Bitsy Carrington Hastings III.

I felt completely alone. I didn't feel at home at Uncle Ben's, with the expensive art and dinner parties and a room that I wasn't allowed to put posters up in. I didn't feel at home at boarding school, where I was tortured on a daily basis. And I didn't feel at home when I visited Mum and Rhiannon, who treated me like a North Shore princess who had picked money over them. I didn't fit in anywhere anymore.

I spent my last year at the College just trying to survive. I stuck to the couple of friends I had in the day school. I even started dating a boy in my last few weeks there. I finished my final exams and aced them, getting into one of the top universities in the country. But my confidence was decimated. I was a ghost, and a ghost can't go to university. A ghost can't make new friends and get a job and speak up in class. A ghost can't live life the way everybody else does. I was still convinced I was being hunted everywhere I went. When I heard people laugh in the street, I thought it was about me. If I saw people whispering in university lectures, I thought they were getting ready to attack. Every corner I turned, I expected a verbal assassin to be waiting for me.

I had no idea how to socially function anymore, and I was exhausted. Fantasising about deformed ball sacks and elaborate penis accidents no longer helped. I was broken.

So, after a month at university, I went to a supermarket and bought a jumbo box of Panadol. The hunters had won – now I was hunting myself.

You will lose your virginity, followed by your mind.

'I peed funny!'

That was the first thing I said after losing my virginity. Once penetration had finally occurred (after weeks of trying, by the way), I got up, went to the bathroom, and looked on in fascination as my pee splayed out of me like someone was holding their finger over the end of a hose. I was mildly concerned I had broken my vagina – after finally figuring out where my tampon hole was, following years of sweating with one leg hoisted on the toilet, had I now stretched things so much that sanitary items would just fall straight out of me anyway? (It should probably be noted here that anybody who thinks tampons can fall out of a vagina because of too much penis-stretching probably shouldn't be having sex to begin with, but such is life.)

The lucky boy was Josh. He was a day student from the College, whom I had started dating during my final few weeks there. After having my confidence and dignity obliterated by

162

kids in the boarding house, I was pretty much left with a couple of friends in the day school, and Josh. I knew we were going to be together from our first drunken kiss at a party. It was one of those kisses that was just so perfect, your knees go to mush. At least, that's the way I felt after having only kissed maybe three other boys, all of whom had assaulted my mouth with their tongues and left me traumatised, confused and feeling betrayed by every Disney kiss I'd ever seen.

Actually, a few years later, once I had hit both my twenties and my threshold for putting up with terrible make-out sessions, I taught a clueless guy how to kiss. It is possibly one of the more selfless and heroic things I have ever done, and ever will do, for humanity. I mean, when you're kids, it's understandable – you're still figuring your shit out. But a grown man not knowing how to kiss a woman without making her want to regurgitate into his mouth? Something had to be done.

I met the random guy at a club (this was during the brief period when I tried doing things other than drink wine at home in my underpants), and it was one of those situations where it was obvious from the second we started talking to each other that we were going to make out.

We exchanged a few obligatory, drunken pleasantries, but as is the way with random hook-ups that take place on a seedy club bench at 2am, subtlety was not really on the cards. One second we were talking, the next we were lunging at each other's faces.

Now, I fully understand that kissing is a subjective thing. Not everybody likes the same technique and it generally takes a few minutes of awkward adjusting before you fall into an acceptable rhythm with someone. But that was not what happened here.

Nothing could have prepared me for the horror that took place in my mouth.

It was like a fat slug had rolled around in mucus and was now trying to mate with my tongue. And the poor little guy couldn't decide where he wanted to go. First he was trying to lick the back of my throat. Then he was trying to coat the entire circumference of my lips with saliva. Then he would somehow lodge himself between my teeth and the side of my cheek.

I had no idea that a tongue could be soft like an oyster and hard like a tampon at the same time. Just as I was trying to deal with my front teeth being attacked in some kind of frenzied stabbing motion, he would change the game on me completely and start trying to fill my mouth with the seemingly never-ending supply of fluid that was secreted from his sex-crazed mucus slug.

I was so thrown by what was happening, I think my brain actually shut down. It wasn't until he took his entire tongue, inserted it as far into my mouth as it would go and then just left it sitting there, perfectly still, that I had a second to think.

This guy needed help, and if I didn't offer it to him, he might subject some poor other girl to his oyster tampon. I couldn't let that happen.

I needed to provide an important public service. And even though I wanted to turn and run with every fibre of my being, I decided to stay. For women everywhere. I was a fucking hero.

I dislodged his mouth from mine and stretched my tongue out a few times.

'Um … what's wrong?' he asked.

'Yeah. We need to talk,' I said. 'That was really, really bad.'

Keep in mind I was pretty inebriated/traumatised at this point, so I wasn't exactly swimming in tact. He seemed genuinely shocked.

'What?!'

'Yeah. Look. You seem really nice. And I can tell you're really trying. But I just can't let you walk away from this … situation thinking that was in any way enjoyable.'

'What?!'

'Have you ever had a girlfriend beyond a few dates?'

'No.'

'And can you think of a time where a girl has been willing to kiss you for more than a few minutes straight?'

It was starting to dawn on him.

'Um … no.'

'It's okay,' I said, feeling more and more like a saviour/Oprah as time went on. I put a hand on his shoulder and looked into his eyes like the hero that I was: 'I can help you.'

I then spent about forty-five minutes with this guy, taking things right back to basics. Literally – basics. I actually had to explain that noses are not a part of the face that need to be taken entirely into the mouth.

We also covered the basic functionality of the tongue, and explored the idea that just because you think yours can reach the back of someone else's throat, doesn't mean you have to prove it.

It was an informative and thorough lesson, and by the end of it he had the basic skills needed to kiss me without making me want to vomit in his mouth. Success.

We practised a few more times, and when I was confident that he was ready to be unleashed on the female population, I let him go. He no doubt remembers me as some kind of wise, selfless demigod. And rightly so.

But back when I was still seventeen, Josh was the first boy I'd ever received a perfect, Disney kiss from. Sure, we were both drunk and sitting in the dirt under the deck at some random kid's house party, but our mouths just connected seamlessly. It was the first time I ever felt that 'Oh my god – nobody on earth could possibly understand that we are just two pieces of a perfect puzzle! Nobody but us has ever felt a love this strong!' kind of feeling. And after that kiss, we were pretty much inseparable.

We spent the next few weeks rubbing up against each other pretty aggressively. Soon the top came off, then the bra, and when we moved on to make-out sessions in just our knickers I knew it was time. There was nowhere else to go but … in. And don't get me wrong – I really wanted to do it, but I was a little scared. Considering I still thought I only had one hole for wee and one hole for poop, I wasn't exactly well acquainted with whatever my situation was down there, let alone his weird-looking bits.

It wasn't particularly magical when we gave it the go-ahead. It was the middle of the day and we'd somehow transitioned from watching *Judge Judy* into some heavy, almost-naked petting.

'Wanna do it?' I said. (Always the classy romantic.)

He acted sufficiently concerned about whether or not I was ready, although I'm certain that inwardly he was crying tears of joy for the balls that over the last few weeks had begun to turn blue in frustration.

So, having begun the beautiful journey of giving up my flower by asking if we should 'do it', it was time to talk protection. I was on the pill already for my skin, but as sexual interns, we felt we needed more. I remembered seeing condoms in the upstairs bathroom, so we decided on that plan of action.

That's where things took a turn.

I think we both assumed that condoms were a one-size-fits-all situation. (Did I mention we were seventeen?) Anyway, after taking ten minutes to pry one out of its plastic-packet fortress, he went to put it on and … well … let's just say whoever had hidden these condoms in the upstairs bathroom was not as well endowed as the young man currently in my bed.

Josh had tried to put a tiny-penis condom on his massive penis, and it got stuck. Halfway down. It wasn't going any further and it wasn't coming back up. That thing was on tight, like rubber-band tight. But we both assumed it was meant to be tight and if we just … kept … forcing it … Bad move. The first love of my life now officially had a latex ring of torture stuck on his dick.

Panic took hold of the room. I suggested scissors. He suggested scissors would go nowhere near his penis. I felt helpless, watching him hop around the room naked with tears streaming down his face. My next mistake? Deciding this was the time to mention that my dad had once told me that cutting off blood flow like this was how farmers get lambs' tails to fall off.

He hurled himself onto the bed. I approached, not realising my naked body was only making the problem worse (you mean they can't control when it moves?). 'Put your freaking top back on!' he yelled.

'Just stay fucking calm!' I yelled back, struggling with my jumper.

We sat in silence for about thirty seconds, both staring down at his possibly-about-to-fall-off dick. Eventually, mercifully, as his boner went down, the killer condom loosened. As soon as it seemed safe, I reached down and yanked it off.

It was the most intimate I had ever been with a penis.

Clearly, we had experienced a false start, but that wasn't going to stop us from trying again. (Not that day, obviously, the remainder of which I spent stroking his head while he lay in the foetal position.)

It actually took a few more tries – I think the initial scare had caused me to close up shop. And when it finally did happen, it was kind of by accident. We were in the midst of another make-out session when it just … slipped in. It hurt, definitely, but I think eventually, it gets to a point where the desire to make contact outweighs the fear of having a massive foreign entity jammed inside you, so you just do it.

I can't even remember the rest. The first thing I do remember is going to the toilet and laughing hysterically because my wee came out like a floodgate had been opened. And not yet understanding that a woman needs some mystique about her, I came running back into the bedroom screaming, 'I peed funny! I peed funny!' A true class act.

After that, Josh and I were basically at it like rabbits on ecstasy. We tried everything and we tried it every which way. In the few months before university started, we pretty much just went to each other's houses and had sex. Sex, cuddles, movie, eat, sleep, repeat. It was heaven. He told me he loved me, and for the first time in my life, I started to have the disastrous thought that a boyfriend could fill the void that my lack of a proper family had left. Josh became my everything. He had a perfect family and lived in a perfect house with a four-wheel drive and a dog. His mum made spaghetti bolognaise and I played handball on the street with his brothers. 'Well, this is it,' I thought. 'This is all I need. As long as I'm around Josh, I'll be fine.'

It was the first time I realised that I could use boyfriends like a drug. Why deal with that pesky depression slowly taking over your brain, when it disappears every time you snuggle into your boyfriend's shoulder? Why bother learning to feel strong for yourself, when he can be strong for you?

It was a dangerous attitude to have at seventeen, especially since my mental health was about to turn to fucking jelly. After a childhood of abandonment and three years at a school where my soul was ripped apart, I was dangerously close to a nervous breakdown. And instead of learning how to climb out of that hole for myself, I expected Josh to pull me out. At a time when I should have been learning to save myself, I appointed Josh my saviour. A really fucking unfair thing to do to a seventeen-year-old kid whose penis had recently been trapped in a tiny condom.

But he did it. No questions asked. And after a few months of dating, the nervous breakdown hit. I had been at university for about a month, studying psychology, living in a tiny room by myself on campus, and everything was catching up with me. My dad. My mum. The violence, the moving, the abuse, the neglect, the death. The fact that I had left Tayla alone. What I had gone through at boarding school. My brain began to completely malfunction, and I was terrified. I had no idea what was happening to me. Instead of going to class, I would sit in my room alone all day and think about ways to kill myself. There were so many memories I couldn't get out of my head. I'd be taking a shower and all of a sudden I'd remember the blood from the night of the Olympics Opening Ceremony. I'd be watching TV and my brain would be taken over with the sounds of my grandpa screaming as my dad beat him. I'd go to spread Vegemite on my toast and see the flash of the knife my mum plunged through Rhiannon's and my bedroom door. I'd walk outside and hear people laughing, and become convinced that Wayne had tracked me down.

If I wasn't spending the day at Josh's house, I would lie in bed in my tiny campus room, staring at the ceiling, trying to get my brain to stop thinking horrific thoughts. That's the trouble with making a person your drug of choice – you can't control when you get a dose. Believe me, I tried. I started to become more and more demanding of his time. He began missing a lot of class, just so he could be with me. I would call him in hysterics, not being able to explain what was wrong except that I couldn't turn my brain off. I just wanted to turn my brain off. And Josh would come, as often as he could. He would take me to his house, where I would have dinner with his parents and seem normal and happy because I was all dosed up for the day. Then he'd drop me back at campus, the drug would wear off, and I'd be calling him within hours begging him to come back to me and make the thoughts stop.

Of course, he couldn't always be there. And that made me irrationally furious. I had spent a lifetime being abandoned, and now here was this boy, the boy I had chosen, the boy who said he loved me, and he couldn't be there for me every time I asked? Whenever he told me that he was sorry but he had class, or he had to spend time with his friends or family, I got the same feeling I used to get when my mum didn't come home.

I had appointed Josh my saviour, my family, my drug. And even though it was spectacularly unfair (not to mention unhealthy for both of us), I expected him to be there for me, and felt let down every time he wasn't. He had the entire weight of repairing the damage of my childhood resting on his shoulders, and that is too damn much for a teenager to deal with. He was the only one who could make the thoughts stop. He was the only one who could make me feel happy, however fleetingly.

So, it's not surprising that it was when Josh was busy one day that I decided to kill myself. It wasn't specifically because I couldn't see him but because he was my heroin, and when he wasn't around, pain took over my entire body. When he wasn't around, all that existed were memories and darkness.

I wasn't exactly sure how one kills oneself. I remember googling 'suicide' and being really annoyed when it just came back with a bunch of websites telling me not to go through with it. I knew I didn't want it to hurt, because I'm a massive wuss and the idea of pain scared me. All I knew was that I wanted it to stop.

All the memories. All the thoughts. All the pain. I wanted to go to sleep and never wake up. Eventually, after sifting through pages of search results with helplines and stories of redemption, I read somewhere that if you take a bunch of headache pills, you'll just fall asleep and die. 'Perfect,' I thought. 'That's what I'll do.' That saved me from having to do something messy or painful, and it seemed easy. I couldn't help but laugh that not only was I taking the 'easy way out', I wanted it to be the easiest easy way out.

I walked to the local supermarket and bought the biggest box of paracetamol they had. I think there were forty-eight in there. I was about to head to the check-out when, for some reason, I decided that if I was just buying the paracetamol, the staff would assume I was up to something suss. I don't know what I expected – maybe a SWAT team of mental-health professionals to suddenly surround me at the counter, telling me to step away from the headache tablets. I guess when you know you're doing something major, your brain assumes that everybody else can tell. Not unlike when you're trying to download music illegally at work. So, to throw the staff off the scent, I also bought a dustpan and brush and some mascara. I have believed every promise ever made to me by every new mascara ever released, and this one promised thickness *and* length, so I could hardly refuse. The dustpan and brush was just because it was something I'd been meaning to buy for a while, it was on sale and I could hardly pass up a bargain – impending suicide or not.

Items successfully purchased without suspicion, I went back to my room, put on the new mascara (which was exactly the same as every other mascara I'd ever tried), and poured myself a big glass of water. I popped every single tablet out of the blister pack and put them in a pile on my bed. Taking them one by one seemed a little over-dramatic, so I just picked them up in handfuls and swallowed them. After five handfuls, I was done. I had killed myself. I sat on the bed for a while, surprised at how easy it was. Now all I had to do was lie down and go to sleep. So that's what I did.

'Motherfucker.' That's the first thought that entered my mind when I woke up. 'Motherfucking fuck tits.' I was tired, and my head hurt (which seems unfair given I had taken forty-eight headache tablets), but I could definitely feel my body and it was definitely alive. I had failed at killing myself. I was the New Coke of suicide attempts.

Assuming I hadn't taken enough, I planned to get up and go and buy two boxes this time – and perhaps another mascara. Then I looked at my phone and realised I'd been asleep for something like twenty hours. I had a bunch of missed calls from Josh. A warm rush came over me. 'Oh, that's right,' I thought. 'Josh.' If he could be my drug that day, I could put the suicide thing off for twenty-four hours. As long as I didn't have to think the thoughts and remember the memories for a while, I'd be okay.

I told Josh what I had done. He freaked out, but he didn't leave. He made me admit to my uncle that I wasn't handling university and needed to leave. My uncle sent me to a psychiatrist who explained that I had post-traumatic stress disorder, and was suffering the fairly common effects of a traumatic childhood like mine. I was put on medication and started going to weekly therapy. But still, I was only at the very beginning of a long journey to repair the damage my life so far had caused my brain. Going to therapy and taking a pill every day doesn't automatically fix things. In fact, for me, things were going to get a lot fucking worse before they got any better. Especially after Josh and I finally broke up.

We stayed together for almost three years after high school, and despite my getting treatment; he was still the strongest and most effective drug I had. Being with Josh meant I didn't have to really try and deal with my problems, because the second I walked out of a therapy session, I could just walk straight into his arms and ignore every difficult thing I'd just talked about. We were in a bubble, and if I was ever going to get better, I needed it to burst.

The break-up began as most first-love break-ups tend to do. We were young, it was the first serious relationship for both of us, and we were just growing apart. I was really only staying with him because of how he made me feel. He had become my only family, and I worried about how I'd handle life without him. He was really only staying with me out of a sense of duty. He knew he had become my only family, and he worried about how I'd handle life without him. We certainly still loved each other, but the love had changed. We would literally shit in front of each other in the bathroom. It was like we had taken one step too far towards 'family' and one step too far away from 'romance'.

We started to fight about lots of little things, ridiculous things. We were constantly bickering. So, it didn't surprise me that after everything we'd been through together, the whole thing would implode over something so stupid. In the end, our relationship ended because of a bike.

A bike was what finally pushed both of us over the edge.

Allow me to explain. Josh still lived with his parents, which, given my desperation for a family, I loved. But he also couldn't drive, and his parents lived about seven fucking kilometres from the train station. So getting to Josh's house took a lot of effort.

When we first got together and there was all the romance and sparkly heart feelings, he would do the round trip. He'd walk the seven kilometres to come and meet me, and then walk seven kilometres with me home. All so I wouldn't have to walk to his place on my own. That's true love.

Then we started using the bike.

We figured out that if we put footpegs on the back of his little brother's bike, he could ride out to meet me in half the time, then I could just stand on the footpegs and hang on for dear life the whole way home.

Two twenty-year-olds cramming on to a twelve-year-old boy's bike because neither of us could drive. I forgot to mention that we were really fucking awesome.

One night, after a particularly crappy day working in my particularly crappy retail job, I begged him to come and meet me with the bike. I wanted to see him, but I didn't want to see him enough to walk seven kilometres after being on my feet for nine hours. He promised that if I came over, he would meet me – bike at the ready.

I got to the station. He wasn't there.

I waited. And waited. And waited.

Half an hour passed – half an hour that I spent thinking about every single annoying thing he had ever done. Half an hour that I spent fuming over the time he didn't come to that dinner, the time he was late to that thing, the time he didn't listen when I talked about that girl, the time he planned a night out when we were meant to see my friends.

Then I started thinking about the bigger things – how he was so unmotivated, how he still lived with his parents, how he didn't know what he wanted to do in life and WHERE IS HE AND WHY THE FUCK CAN'T HE DRIVE?

It was right at the point my brain started thinking in capital letters that he arrived.

He didn't stand a chance.

'Don't even talk to me,' I said. 'Let's just go.'

It was when I went to get on the back of the bike that everything came crashing down.

'Where are the footpegs?' I asked, with a level of calm that shocked even me.

'Oh … shit,' he replied. The fear in his voice was obvious.

We spent the next two hours on the side of the road arguing about our relationship under the guise of the bike. How could he forget the footpegs? Why was I overreacting about the footpegs? Why was he late? Why hadn't I been clear about the time? Why did he always make me feel bad about being busy? Why did I always expect him to read my mind? How could he be so disorganised? Stop trying to change the subject, *this is about the bike.*

Obviously, it wasn't about the bike.

We broke up three days later. After years of being focussed on playing our designated roles – him the saviour and me the saved, we hadn't noticed that we actually didn't have a lot in common. We actually really gave each other the shits on an epic scale, but the task of making sure I was okay meant we never really thought about it.

We agreed to go our separate ways, and at first, it was mutual. We were sitting by the water at Darling Harbour, and we both hugged and cried and said our goodbyes.

But two days later, I cracked. I wanted him back. I began to panic. I would listen to Missy Higgins for hours while snot-crying into a wine glass. I invented a fake MySpace profile so I could spy on him and see if he was out with any girls. I called him, relentlessly.

But luckily, Josh stood firm. I think he knew better than I did that I only wanted him back because I was too scared to be alone. And despite begging him to take me back in an increasingly humiliating myriad of ways, he wouldn't. He had finally realised that I wasn't his responsibility, and he walked away.

It was the greatest gift he could ever have given me. I needed to learn how to function emotionally on my own. I needed to realise that I had the strength to survive without a man to hide behind. It was going to take me a long time to learn – there would be another attempt at making a boy my drug and a stay in a mental institution before I really hit rock bottom – but Josh was the first one to push me into the deep end of the pool.

And because I wasn't quite ready, I reached out to the only flotation device I could think of besides him – actual drugs (the non-boyfriend kind), and lots of faceless, humiliating sex. I was at the beginning of my adult self-destruction.

You will go to a very crappy drama school and do a very crappy naked scene.

I knew that I would chicken out. I knew, all the way through the rehearsal, and all day before the first performance, that I wasn't going to do it. As people were looking at me with 'Geez, I couldn't do what you're doing' faces, and friends were patting me on the back wishing me luck, I already had an emergency pair of costume knickerbockers in my bag, because I knew there was no way I was going to go full-nude onstage in front of a theatre full of people.

It was 2006, and I was in my second year at a very crappy drama school. It was the kind of drama school that you didn't actually have to audition for — as long as you had the money to pay them, they would take you. It was in a few crappy rooms in a run-down office building in Surry Hills, but the school also rented a theatre right in the middle of Sydney city, which made us feel really legit. When other, proper drama students would ask us where our campus was, we'd sort of mumble something about

Surry Hills before proclaiming, 'But most of our classes are at the Pilgrim Theatre, you know, on Pitt Street?' Something about the theatre being in the city made us feel like we weren't wasting so much of our money. The kind of students who went there were the ones who'd been rejected from the proper schools – NIDA, WAAPA, VCA – but still had a lot of misplaced enthusiasm. I see some of them pop up in the occasional commercial now, bright-eyed and gung-ho, declaring that the latest Toyota has twelve months of free servicing. At first, it was the kind of thing that made you proud, but almost ten years after graduating, one commercial every two years just feels kind of sad.

I ended up at the Australian Academy of Dramatic Art (abbreviated to AADA, probably in the hope that people might mistake it for NIDA) in 2005. After my disastrous, one-month stint at Sydney University, I spent the rest of the year working in retail, before deciding that all those Oscars speeches I'd practised in my room over the years should probably be given a chance to make it to the actual Oscars stage. I was right at the start of my treatment for PTSD, had just begun taking medication for depression and anxiety, and all I wanted was to do something fun. To be honest, I didn't even try to audition for the proper schools. An audition process seemed way too daunting, and my confidence was shot after being verbally assassinated by Wayne for three years in private-school hell. That AADA wasn't going to force me to audition was the reason I picked it.

There were about thirty students in the freshman year of 2005, and I'd say less than half of those had any kind of talent. Probably about a quarter were embarrassingly bad. So bad that you'd watch them onstage and think, 'How can you not know? How has there been no one kind enough in your life to tell you that every time you open your mouth to act, people are cringing in the dark?' But then you'd think, 'Well, if they don't know, and nobody's told them, maybe I don't know that *I'm* shit, and nobody's told me.' And then you'd generally freak out until you got pissed and convinced yourself that you could definitely get an agent if you just lost a few kilos.

Besides the moderately talented students and the really, really bad students, there was also just a bunch of charismatic kids who had liked drama in high school and weren't really sure what else to do. I'd say I fell into the latter group. I wasn't great; I wasn't terrible — I just wanted to have fun. Of course, since I had not managed to increase my cool quota in the slightest since childhood, my idea of fun was sketch comedy and goofing around. I read gossip mags at lunch while other students were reading Chekhov. I just wanted to make up funny skits; other students wanted to break down the beats in *A Doll's House*.

But drama school was how I found my soul mates. After spending three years at a high school where I walked away with exactly two friends (one of whom was Josh), I needed to find a community. And the kids at drama school who didn't give a fuck gave me that community. We were the ones who laughed about how shit our campus was (and the fact that anyone even tried to call three rooms in an office building a 'campus'). We were the ones who skipped movement class to go and get pissed at the pub. We were the ones who openly admitted that our entire course was probably just a money-making scheme for the dubious owner, and thought that made the whole experience even more hilarious. Basically, the people I was drawn to at drama school were the people who just wanted to laugh at life, and those people remain my friends to this day.

We often spent entire two-hour classes in suspended 'character play'. For one particular class, each student had a chair, which they had to romantically dance with and seduce. For an hour. One guy was so appalled by the ridiculousness of it that he flat-out refused to seduce his chair, which was major sacrilege.

'He *refuses* to dance with the chair?'

'He needs to let go!'

'He's so closed off to his true inner self.'

'He'll never be a truly great actor if he can't spend an hour making love to a piece of furniture.'

In another class, I had trouble spending forty-five minutes living my character's journey as a 'very sexual dolphin'. My acting teacher looked at me with pity, like it was so sad that I didn't have what it took to ever really be a great creative spirit. (I'm quite pleased that, besides the odd McDonald's commercial, nobody who successfully seduced their chair or spent an hour gawking like a parrot has found success either. I KNEW THE CHAIR SEDUCING WAS BULLSHIT.) So, given my propensity to goof around and not really give a toss about spending an hour imagining my character as 'a deaf baby', I was surprised to be offered a pretty dramatic lead role in my second year.

This role came to be known as 'the naked role'. It was highly coveted, since the minute you get naked onstage you are immediately a brave and talented actor. I was going to play a nun. She has fallen in love with Don Juan and given her virginity to him, and when she realises that he's had a bunch of other girls on the side, she rips off her nun's habit in a rush of emotion, because she feels like she no longer has the right to represent God. Then she stands naked in front of Don Juan, crying, before exiting stage left.

Heavy stuff. Heavy stuff that I had no doubt in my mind I would never be able to pull off. The nun was a mostly comedic role, which was why, I assume, it was offered to me, but her last (emotional, naked) scene was the one I knew I wouldn't even come close to getting right. So I just put the scene to the back of my mind – the naked part and the 'quality acting' part. It was probably the best female role in the play, and I was so flattered to have been cast, that I sort of forgot that there was no chance in hell I was ever going to be able to do it.

On the day of our first show, we had a tech run and a dress rehearsal. The director told me that I could stay dressed for those, and that I only had to go full-naked for opening night if I felt comfortable. I told him I definitely would be, knowing that I definitely wouldn't be. There was more chance of me hanging out with the kids who read Chekhov at lunch than there was of me getting naked on that stage.

The sad part of the whole thing was the actual reason I didn't want to get naked. It had nothing to do with people seeing my private parts; I was happy to let my vag hang out in front of a crowd. It was because of my body. I had broken up with Josh about halfway through the year, and since then had gained some weight. Not a lot, but enough to make me feel weird and self-conscious about my body for the first time in my life. I'd always been relatively slim – or at least, not big enough to warrant any kind of serious body-hate – and now I was starting to develop a little belly. A little belly that was giving me a huge amount of fucking insecurity.

It didn't help that a few weeks earlier, after seeing me eat a delicious blueberry bagel smothered in butter from Starbucks, one of my acting teachers pulled me aside and told me she was really concerned 'about my nutrition'. 'You're extremely talented, Rosie,' she said, a patronising hand resting on mine. 'But I worry that in an industry that relies so much on looks, if you don't concentrate on your nutrition, you're not going to get the parts you deserve.' I agonised over that conversation for weeks. I had gained about five kilos after the break-up, nothing to be hugely concerned about. But that conversation set something off in my brain. In fact, the week after she said that to me, I starved myself for the very first time, in what would become a years-long battle with an eating disorder.

So basically, I didn't want to get naked because I was more concerned that people would see my slightly protruding belly than I was about them seeing my vagina. I didn't realise it then, but that was probably the most profound lesson I learned about being a woman in show business in my entire time at drama school.

In the countdown to curtains up, there was a nervous energy backstage. Nobody had seen me naked, and everybody was wondering if I was actually going to do it. In fact, I was already wearing specially made underwear beneath my costume. I had made it myself out of cheap calico, because I couldn't find a pair in the shops that went high enough to cover the belly I had become so obsessed with. Everyone kept wishing me luck for something I knew I had no intention of doing.

Adrian, an arse of a guy who took all the chair-seducing stuff very seriously, even seemed to have a little respect for me. This was surprising, given we'd slept together a few weeks earlier and I'd been so off my face that I'd then proceeded to tell everyone that the sex was awful and he had a tiny penis (he didn't). It had been a slip of the drugged-up tongue, but he still would never forgive me (and rightfully so, to be honest). We were at a friend's twenty-first birthday, which was held at some swanky golf club, and about halfway through the night, it was decided that in order to teach all these rich, swanky golf-club people a lesson, we would sneak down to the eighteenth hole and do a big shit in it. Granted, I was twenty, had very much taken advantage of the open bar and had a couple of pills in my system already, but even as I write this now, sober, I think it's a pretty funny idea.

Adrian and I ran off together into the night, frolicking through the golf course, holding hands and looking for hole number eighteen. I'm not sure either of us knew how to find it, or if we had considered any kind of logistical plan, but before I knew what was what, we were making out on the hole instead of shitting in it. Then we were having sex on the hole instead of shitting in it. I guess that's what happens when you try to shit in a hole while on ecstasy.

Adrian clearly wasn't enjoying himself. I clearly wasn't enjoying myself. But I had been taught that sex was a failure unless the boy comes, so I stubbornly kept at it. Then, my phone rang, and in what seemed like a perfectly reasonable move at the time, I answered it.

'Yesh, Helloing?' I said, continuing to ride Adrian like a sad, lonely seesaw.

'Rosie! It's Tonz! Where the hell are you guys? The party's over, everyone's leaving and going to Club 77!'

'Oh. Um,' I was clearly out of breath.

'Wait, what the fuck Rosie? Are you having sex right now?'

'Um ...'

'Ew! You slut! Hahahahahahahaha! Hey, you guys, Rosie and Adrian are totally doing it! Just meet us here soon – k – bye.'

I threw the phone down and kept going. Adrian had his eyes closed tight, but not in a passionate kind of way. His face looked halfway between concentrating on a maths question and trying not to cry. I climbed off him.

'Okay,' I said, defeated. 'Everyone's left. Are you going to the club?'

'I guess so,' he said, with the attitude of a kid who'd woken up on Christmas morning expecting an iPad and got a new school bag instead.

The entire golf course grounds had been closed, so the next fifteen minutes were spent trying to find a fence we could jump. All in complete silence. We flagged a cab down and rode all the way to the club still in complete silence. I was so off my face, it was only 11pm and I was already holding my shoes. When we finally got to Club 77 and I saw my friends, it was like my mouth erupted with the orgasm I wished Adrian had just had. Details just came exploding out of me.

'You guyyyyysshhh! It was sooooo bad! And his penisy-thingy was teeny-teeny-teeny-tiny! And he didn't even come!

Whattsh wrong with me? Ish that my fault? That can't be my fault! Oh! And oh my gosh, you guysh, it was soooo bad and why didn't he come and his thingy was small.'

It really wasn't. But I was so traumatised by the fact I hadn't been able to make him come that I felt like I needed to save face. Also, the ecstasy was compromising my otherwise tactful brain.

'Rosie. Shut up for a second.' Tonz shoved a glass of water in my face, the drinking of which mercifully kept me quiet for thirty seconds. But it was too late. I turned around. Adrian had been standing there, listening to the whole thing. I felt so bad that I then proceeded to get fingered by another guy on the dance floor right in front of him, to which I'm sure he thought, 'bullet fucking dodged'. Which at that point, I certainly was. Screwing one guy and getting fingered by another in one night was pretty clear evidence that I was not handling my break-up well. My self-esteem was in the toilet, and momentary sexual encounters were giving me a very brief taste of the comfort I had felt with Josh. Of course, the brief comfort that comes from a hook-up like that is cruelly cancelled out when you look back on the night before and realise you only did it because you just wanted to be held by somebody. And coming down off the ecstasy probably doesn't help either.

So, after my drug-fuelled lie to a club full of people about the size of Adrian's peen, I was surprised when he wished me luck for my big scene. I didn't have the heart to tell anyone I was a total fraud.

The first act went fine. I had all my funny lines and stole most of my scenes with the kind of improvising that irritated everyone onstage but got me a lot of laughs from the audience (#teamplayer). During intermission the director came backstage to see if I was okay, and to tell me once again that I didn't have to do it if I didn't want to, to which I once again responded that I definitely would, knowing full well I already had calico undies on beneath my costume.

When the scene got closer, I suddenly remembered the whole 'acting' side of it. I'd been so worried about admitting to anyone that I was too scared to go naked that I'd completely forgotten I also had no freaking chance of reaching the emotional level the scene required. 'Oh god,' I thought, waiting to go on. 'This is going to be fucking humiliating.'

I approached Don Juan, putting as much 'emotion' into the scene as I could by yelling everything I said. All of a sudden I was regretting not taking the chair-seducing classes seriously. *And why the fuck had I refused to be a sexy dolphin?* Why had I laughed at every acting exercise we ever did? Now I was standing onstage, yelling at some guy, feeling no better than Tabitha in *Passions*, and in approximately ten seconds I was going to rip off my nun's habit and disappoint everyone by wearing undies.

I yelled my final, 'this is the cue for the lighting guys that I'm about to get naked' line, adding in what I felt was a very dramatic head turn at the end. Then, in one swift move, I ripped off my nun's habit and stood onstage. Brave, defiant, broken, naked. Except in my undies.

In fairness to me, I was fully topless, so at least my tits were out for all to see. I hoped that at least made me *half* a brave actor. To be honest, I was just relieved that nobody saw my little belly. I had strategically ripped the undies in certain places so that some people might get a bit of a look at my vag, but mostly I chickened out of a nude scene, because I was embarrassed about not having a six-pack. Like nuns have six-packs anyway.

I was never offered another lead role after that, and left drama school halfway through my final year because I couldn't afford the ridiculous fees anymore. I was sad not to graduate, but I hardly think it made a difference to my career. A year later I enrolled at the University of Technology, Sydney, to study creative writing, and realised that's probably what I should have been concentrating on all along. All I'd ever wanted to do was write funny skits and perform them, without the pressure of meeting an emotional crescendo that warrants the ripping off of a nun's habit. I just wanted acting to be fun. And my idea of fun was not seducing chairs and pretending to be a sexy dolphin. Although that would make a great fucking skit.

Your second set of parents will abandon you. Damn.

When I was nineteen, I peed my pants in Coles. Granted, I was a little (very) intoxicated. I hadn't yet built up the kind of tolerance that comes from the regular consumption of cheap vodka and even cheaper wine. I was at a party within walking distance of my house, and I managed to convince the long-suffering Josh that I could get from said party to my bedroom on my own with no hassles or delays.

So off I trotted, heels in hand, headed towards a warm bed (by which I obviously mean the crawl space next to the toilet). What Josh didn't count on was there being a Coles between point A and point B. And everybody knows that when walking home from a big night, Drunk Brain takes over Regular Brain and leads the body towards food instead of home.

I can't remember the exact details, but what I do know is this: at some point during what should have been a five-minute walk, I ended up in Coles looking for crumpets and Fanta. And I peed my pants.

It was pretty close to closing time, and I must have looked an absolute mess, because the security guard stared me down with a worried/puzzled look on his face the second I walked in the door. Of course, Drunk Brain assumed he was staring at me because I looked fabulous, and that put a pretty confident spring in my step. The fact I was carrying my heels instead of wearing them, and one of my false lashes was dangling off my face, also didn't register with me. I sauntered through that entrance like I was walking a red carpet.

I then proceeded to aimlessly wander the aisles for twenty minutes.

It was somewhere between deciding on the crumpets but still not sure about the Fanta that I got the feeling. Like my bladder was suddenly, and out of nowhere, overflowing to the point where it had decided to start pushing out liquid whether I agreed to it or not. *That* feeling.

I ignored it at first, and continued with the more pressing decision of which fizzy drink I should buy and cuddle up with in bed. (And again, if the story includes me being drunk, feel free to assume the word 'bed' means 'toilet'.) But it got worse. And worse. I even tried that subtle manoeuvre of pretending I was looking at something on the bottom shelf so I could crouch down and try to use my foot as a plug, but to no avail. This wee was happening. And it was happening now.

At this point I had three options: I could leave immediately, find some bushes outside and do my business; I could go right there in the aisle, which although a public place, I currently had to myself; or, option number three, I could attempt the impossible feat of reversing a waterfall, proceed to the counter and buy my desperately needed items, risking the very real possibility I would wet myself in front of a security guard and terrified check-out guy.

It was 2am and I was crouching down in the dog food aisle with no shoes on. A decision clearly needed to be made. Guess which option Drunk Brain chose?

I proceeded to the check-out, with what I estimated was about thirty seconds before the urine dam exploded. Of course at this point the manager entered the scene, and decided it was imperative he count every five-cent coin ever placed into circulation and put them into little bags.

That was obviously the moment a sane individual would have made a run for it. But damn it, it had taken me twenty minutes to decide I wanted those crumpets, and I wasn't leaving without them.

So with the security guard, manager and check-out guy all within ten feet of me, I carried out what I thought was the only viable option left. With my crumpets and heels in one hand and Fanta in the other, I decided to let that wee flow as discreetly as possible. Drunk Brain reasoned that I really wanted those crumpets, and the chances of anybody noticing were slim. Drunk Brain was wrong.

You know when you've been busting to wee for such a long time that when you finally get to go, it just keeps coming and coming? And coming? This was one of those times. Finally opening the floodgates was beyond satisfying, but within two seconds it was clear that this was no discreet operation. As the warm liquid ran down my leg and formed a puddle on the floor, I think the four of us in that Coles shared an oddly intimate moment. First, they couldn't take their eyes off me. Then they stared at each other in equal parts horror and disbelief. Then back to me. And all the while I just stood there, like I was any normal lady waiting in a supermarket line, absolutely not doing a wee.

When the stream finally receded, the manager was the first to snap out of our shared trance. 'Can I help you?' he asked, as he motioned me over. 'Yes, thank you,' I replied, as I held my head high and walked slowly over to the counter with an air of importance (evidently, Drunk Brain had decided the only way out of this was to maintain my dignity by acting well above my station), all the while leaving wet footprints in my wake. 'I'd like to purchase these, please,' I said with a head toss. All three of them continued to stare at me. It was like I was a crazy person with a bomb and nobody wanted to do anything that would make me nervous.

Everything was a little anti-climactic after that; I just paid for my crumpets and Fanta and sashayed out of there. I didn't look back, but I'm certain the three of them stood there in shocked silence for at least another minute. Then they had to decide who was taking care of that puddle. I wet my pants in Coles, and didn't leave until I had bought my crumpets.

Less than two years later, my uncle and aunt asked me to leave their home. I always wondered if they'd somehow discovered I had wet my pants at the local supermarket.

My uncle and aunt, Ben and Natasha, were crazy wealthy. They lived in a huge mansion that was like a museum – it was very clean and there was lots of expensive art that you weren't allowed to touch. Everything was white and open plan. Spilling a drink on the carpet was considered an emergency on par with a natural disaster. My uncle would spring into action with about ten different products, all the while swearing and making me feel like I'd caused thousands of dollars worth of damage with one glass of Coke. Come to think of it, given the cost of everything in their home, I probably had.

I had lived with Ben and Natasha for a little while when I was a kid, but when I went to live with them permanently at fourteen, they sent me straight to boarding school. So, for three years, I was living with them without really living with them.

All I really knew was that I wasn't allowed to put posters on my wall, and they had a dog they loved more than me. His name was Hamish, he was a West Highland white terrier, and as a rich couple with no kids, they treated him like their one true son and heir.

I fucking hated that dog. And rightfully so – he was awful. He wasn't friendly. He wasn't affectionate. I think he's the only dog I've met in my entire life who didn't like to hug. He used to bite little kids, then Ben and Natasha would get angry with the kids for 'provoking' him. He walked around with a sense of entitlement that pissed me off – it reminded me of the boys at boarding school. It was like he knew I didn't belong. Whenever he looked at me, I just imagined him thinking, 'Ugh, you're that Houso kid who belongs to my dad's drunk sister. Why are you here taking up my place on the couch, you commoner?'

Hamish was walked three times a day and given gourmet meals. In fact, I often got a smaller portion than everyone else at dinner 'so that Hamish wouldn't feel left out'. 'I'll fucking leave your stupid face out,' I used to think, as Ben and Natasha each chomped down on two chorizo sausages, and I looked at my second one sitting in Hamish's bowl.

He was basically just an all-round smug piece of shit on four legs, and I hated that my new parents always seemed more excited about having him around than me. I got back at him in small, secret ways, though. When I spilled drinks on the carpet while I was home alone, I would cover it in the cleaning powder and then say Hamish had done a shit. Or when I was meant to take him to the park, I would walk him just far enough down the road to see the park, then I would turn around and drag him home. Ours was a fairly disturbing – although in my opinion equal – sibling rivalry.

But mostly I was at boarding school, so I could handle the uncomfortable life I had at the museum house with the shitty excuse for a dog. Just when I felt like I couldn't handle another second at school, I got to go home for the holidays. Then, just when I felt like I couldn't handle another second in a home that wasn't really mine, I got to go back to school. Until, of course, I finished high school, which meant living at home permanently.

In the three years I'd spent living at the College, the bullying I'd experienced had taken a lot out of me. When I finally escaped that situation and had time to decompress, the depression, anxiety and PTSD started. I mostly relied on Josh to get me through it, but that didn't stop Ben and Natasha from wondering what the hell had happened to the promising young bookworm they'd sent to boarding school three years earlier. I was withdrawn, quiet, weird. I'd stay at Josh's for days at a time. I dropped out of university after a month. They never knew that I had tried to kill myself, but they did see I was depressed, and they paid for me to go to therapy, which was incredibly generous of them.

I think they thought that throwing money at the problem was going to fix it, but it wasn't that easy. My first suicide attempt after boarding school was only the beginning of the long and difficult journey of dealing with my childhood trauma, and I was not easy to deal with during that journey. By the time Josh and I broke up, Ben and Natasha were married and had two kids of their own, and were itching to live life as a family. A family that didn't include the weird, withdrawn niece who dropped out of uni and hid in her room all the time. I was the odd one out. The 'spot the random'. They had promised to be my parents, but I could feel them pulling away.

I first realised they were frustrated when Natasha approached me about my therapy one day. 'So, Rosie,' she asked. 'How much longer do you think you'll be going to the psychiatrist for?'

'Um, I don't know,' I replied hesitantly. 'I hadn't really thought about it.'

'It's really expensive, you know.'

'I know,' I said.

'And you've been going for two years now. Isn't it time to start winding it up?'

I stood in silence, a little gobsmacked. Was she telling me I had to give up therapy? Was she telling me they were sick of paying for it?

'We help you pay for drama school. We pay for all your psychiatrist sessions. You live here for free. It's a lot, you know.'

After that conversation, I freaked out. I wanted to be what they wanted, happy and together and successful and perfect. But I couldn't do it. I tried, but I just couldn't do it. The memories and the thoughts would always come back. The knife under the door. Dad in the back of the paddy wagon. Grandpa screaming. I couldn't get my brain to do what I wanted it to do, and even though I knew it frustrated Ben and Natasha that I was so different from what they had hoped for, I just didn't feel I could control it.

The more I felt them pushing me away, the more anxious I became. I started trying to be a cool kid with the wrong kinds of people. Every weekend involved getting wasted, and often fucking some guy in a bathroom. I just so badly wanted to feel wanted, I would hook up with whoever would take me. I got home one night in the middle of winter and realised I had forgotten my key, but rather than wake up Ben and get in trouble, I slept on the doorstep, under the doormat for warmth. I had a bunch of friends stay over while Ben and Natasha and the kids were away, and a few days later Natasha noticed that money was missing from one of the girls' moneyboxes. Those were the kinds of 'cool kids' I was hanging out with.

The hard partying was making my depression and anxiety worse. I had a job and went to drama school, but when I was at home I just hid in my room, crying and sleeping, staring at the walls, watching hours of TV then having no memory of what I'd seen. I had fallen into a cycle of binging and purging and starving myself, so I was hiding food and vomit all over my room. I started having panic attacks in class. I was falling to pieces without Josh.

And Ben and Natasha had no freaking clue what was going on. I feel for them, I really do. I was severely depressed, and can't have been easy to live with. To them, I think it just seemed like I was a belligerent, self-destructive twenty-year-old, with no gratitude for everything they'd done for me.

The last straw was when I got my period all over an expensive pair of Natasha's undies. When you're constantly fighting thoughts of suicide, you hardly think about doing washing, so I snuck into Natasha's wardrobe one day and took a pair of her knickers. And of course, when you've borrowed someone else's knickers, the universe decides to unexpectedly give you your period so you get blood all over them. I freaked out. These were nice, expensive undies. And I had wrecked them. There's no way the stains were going to wash out. So, I hid them in my room and hoped that Natasha would forget she'd ever owned them.

She didn't forget.

I came home from work late one night and found an envelope taped to my bedroom door. Inside was a letter from Ben, about five pages long, listing all the things that he and Natasha were pissed off at me about. All the things I had been doing wrong. All the ways in which I was selfish and awful to live with. Staying out late. Being withdrawn. Not doing my dishes. Never talking to them. Sleeping all day. Taking Natasha's undies and staining them with period blood.

The letter was fair. Everything he said in it was true. He may not have taken the time to try and understand the causes of my behaviour, but everything he said was accurate, and that sent me into a total meltdown. I don't think I said one word to either of them for the next two weeks. I could feel my second set of parents slipping away, and one wrong move was going to destroy everything. I figured if I could just stay out of their way and try not to fuck anything up, I wouldn't piss them off again and they wouldn't ask me to go.

Then they asked me to go.

I was in my room after drama school one night. Door closed as usual. Ben came and knocked on the door, which he never, ever did. I answered it, and he stood in the doorway almost like my room was not really part of the house, and he felt awkward coming in.

'Look, Rosie, we need to talk about your living arrangements,' he said.

My heart sank. This was it. I'd ruined everything.

'You know that we're moving out to renovate soon,' he said.

'Yeah?' I replied, hoping that he was about to tell me we'd just be moving house for a while.

'Well, I just thought you should know that Natasha and the girls and I won't be taking you with us, so you're going to have to organise somewhere else to live.'

Natasha and the girls. I had always hoped I was one of the girls.

'Oh. Okay,' I replied. I didn't know what to say.

'We can help you financially while you get on your feet, but you should know that this is going to be a permanent thing. When the house is done, we don't plan on having a room for you here.'

'Oh.' I could feel the toxic butterflies awakening.

'So, you should probably start looking for something as soon as possible,' he said.

'Okay.'

He walked away. I shut the door and went and sat on my bed, in shock. I'd come to live with them when I was fourteen and I was now twenty. That's almost seven years, a longer consecutive period of time than I'd ever lived with my mum. I considered Ben and Natasha my family, and I'd just been told that they considered me nothing more than a person who lived in their house and soon no longer would.

I packed a bag and left the house about five minutes after that conversation. I never spent another night there. I went to stay with Rhiannon, sleeping on her couch. A few weeks later, we drove to Ben and Natasha's to pick up my stuff. They had dumped everything on the porch and used my doona to cover it all from the rain. It smelled like it had been out there for a while.

I never heard from them again. They never called to check if I was okay. They never called to see where I had ended up. It was like I had never been a part of their lives. I bet Hamish was fucking thrilled.

I spent the next year couch-hopping. I stayed with Rhiannon for a while, I stayed with Mum for a while, I stayed with friends for a while. I was lost and alone, and had nowhere to go. I knew what I needed. I needed another boy to save me.

You will end up in a
mental institution.

When a guy wearing nothing but a bedsheet as a toga pushes in front of you in the dinner line so he can get better dibs on the custard, you know you've hit rock bottom.

I was twenty-four, and I was in a mental institution. Pretty much nailing life.

It all began when I found the boy. The perfect, funny, good-looking boy. My year-long destructive partying phase was over, and I was looking for a distraction that was more permanent. I didn't want to just have sex in club toilets or do a line of coke to make the thoughts go away – that high never lasted long enough. What I needed was another Josh. I needed another boy to make me feel loved.

Of course, what I really needed was to learn how to love myself. To learn how to survive on my own and to actually face the pain and trauma from my past. But I had been through too much for one damn year, so when Luka told me he loved me, that he wanted to marry me and have my babies, I gladly let myself be enveloped by it. If only I'd known that less than two years later, I'd be hustling in a dinner line at a mental home. And I don't even *like* custard.

Luka and I met at the movies. We both worked there with a bunch of other uni students and creative people, making popcorn and cleaning out the slushie machines. After couch-hopping for what seemed like an eternity, I moved into a share-house in Chippendale with a few other cinema staff. On my first night there, Luka stayed over, and he kissed me. 'So, um, I kind of like you,' he said, in his charmingly geeky way. 'I kind of like you too,' I replied, and we kissed again.

It would have been the perfect romantic moment if Luka hadn't already had a girlfriend. Kissing him that night was probably one of the worst things I've ever done, but I was so desperate to be loved that my usual moral compass was pointing only towards him. He had left every girl he'd ever been with for another, and in the back of my mind that worried me, but he promised me that I was different. He'd cheated on or lied to all those girls because he was confused or didn't care about them, but he *knew* he wanted to be with me. He could see a future with me. I was the girl he loved. And I believed him. He said every exact thing that I'd ever wanted to hear from a guy. I was intoxicated from the second he said 'family' and kissed me on the nose.

I was smart enough to know that I shouldn't be getting into any kind of relationship. After relying on Josh, then relying on drugs and random sex, it was time that I learned how to rely on myself. I was also smart enough to know that any guy who cheats on someone else to be with you is eventually going to cheat on you to be with someone else. But the lure of a warm hug from a man who could make me forget my problems was too tempting to let go, even if he was an arsehole.

And, although I didn't realise it at the time, an arsehole was exactly what I needed. My desperation to be loved needed to come up against someone so selfish and shitty that it would force me into total meltdown. I needed a disaster to push me down to rock bottom, so that I could finally learn how to claw my own way out and build my own life.

Luka was that disaster.

The first warning sign was that he said he loved me after a week, which, believe me, is never, ever true. Someone telling you they love you when you've only been dating a week is like someone telling you they like *Two and a Half Men* when they've only seen the opening credits. It's a very big – and very misguided – call to make. There is just a whole lot more horrible shit coming that you couldn't possibly anticipate from only seeing the fun beginning. You only really know if love is there once you've waded through the mess and are still interested in sticking around.

Other warning signs came thick and fast. We had to keep our relationship a secret for the first few months, because he didn't want anyone to know that he'd left his previous girlfriend to be with me. When I eventually snapped and told people, he said I was selfish, and I had to promise to give him one head job a day forever to get him to stay with me. It was my suggestion, and although half-joking, I was still only *half*-joking. That's how fucking desperate I was. He wasn't interested in hearing about my family or my background because it made him 'uncomfortable'. He seemed exasperated by my anxiety and depression. He would often belittle me in front of his friends.

Basically, Luka was just a young, selfish guy. He could be very sweet, but he always cared about his needs first, and since he had cheated on someone to be with me, I was just waiting for him to betray me in the same way. I had picked a saviour who was guaranteed to abandon me. Subconsciously I must have known things needed to explode, and he was the perfect dynamite.

After the first few months, when I could tell that his interest in me was waning, I panicked. I couldn't handle losing yet another promise of a family. And just like when I felt my mum pull away, and when I felt Josh pull away, and when I felt my aunt and uncle pull away, my body went into battle mode.

My mental health began to deteriorate pretty rapidly. I was cutting myself. My eating disorder was out of control and I was gaining a lot of weight. If Luka didn't text me back after ten minutes, I became convinced he was with another girl. I was having constant panic attacks and I expected him to drop everything to help me fix the problem. I took to spending hours sitting in my wardrobe, because even the open space of my bedroom made me nervous. I attempted suicide two more times, all because Luka wouldn't answer the phone or would leave my house after an argument. I just couldn't face the pain of being alone and having the thoughts and memories come back.

I was falling apart, and Luka realised a lot quicker than Josh had that he didn't want any part of it. But just like with all his previous girlfriends, he was too scared to leave me until he'd found someone else. He said he wasn't sure if he loved me anymore and that he needed to take a break. I naïvely took that to mean, 'I definitely love you, I just need some time to remember that.' What he actually meant was, 'I definitely don't love you anymore, but there's this girl at work that I like and I want to see how that goes before I completely cut you loose.'

We spent about a month being together but not really being together. I would sleep with him whenever he wanted; partly because I craved closeness and partly because I thought it would make him love me (sidenote: having sex with a guy who doesn't love you will not make him love you). The awful thing about the sex during that month was that he refused to kiss me. It seemed like his way of reminding me that he hadn't 'decided' yet. Like a sexual disclaimer: you can't get mad at me for sleeping with you because I made it clear with the no-kissing thing that it was just sex.

He called me, really drunk one night at 3am, and told me that he missed me and just wanted to be with me. He came to my house, said he was an idiot for ever letting me go, and then passed out on my bed. I spent the night physically holding his arms around me, nuzzling my head into his drunken, snoring face. Something in me knew that in the morning he would take it back, and I just wanted to be held before it was over, even if I had to hold his arms there myself. In the morning, he took it back.

A few weeks later he admitted that he'd been seeing a girl from work, and now she was leaving her boyfriend so they could be together. Oh, and he'd also finally decided that he definitely wasn't in love with me. I let out a scream of pain down the phone that shocked even me. I'd had no idea my body could make a sound like that. He told me it was unfair of me to be angry, since technically he had broken up with me over a month ago. And technically that was true. But it was a shitty technicality. A technicality that I knew was going to come back and haunt me every time I remembered he had been willing to put his dick in me, but refused to kiss me.

I was alone again, and it was my fault. Luka had been selfish, definitely, but I had also pushed him away with my craziness and panic attacks and trust issues and cutting and suicidal thoughts and crying and memories.

I couldn't imagine ever finding one person in my life who wouldn't leave. All I wanted was to swallow every pill I could find and die, which had become my usual go-to plan at that point. But I decided to try something different that day. I knew I wanted to die because I wanted the pain to stop, so maybe if I got the pain to stop, I wouldn't have to die. I sat on my bed, a pile of pills on the doona in front of me, and instead of picking them up and swallowing them, I called my sister and told her I was suicidal. I told her I needed help. I told her that I was thinking about death and I wanted it to stop, and I was worried that if it didn't stop soon I would try it again.

She came and picked me up. I was in my pyjamas and could barely move. I was panicking and hysterical. She took me to the emergency room, where we waited for hours. A fairly exasperated nurse assessed me.

'So, what's the problem?'

I could hardly speak. 'Um, I'm feeling really suicidal, and I'm worried about what I'll do.'

'What was that? Can you speak up?' she snapped, getting distracted by something going on in another room.

'I'm, um, suicidal.'

'But you haven't attempted?'

I didn't quite know how to answer that question. This was getting too hard. All I wanted to do was go home and swallow a bunch of pills and go to sleep forever. 'Well, I have before, but not today.'

'So you didn't feel bad enough this time that you decided to go through with it today?'

'Well, no, I did. It's just, I'm worried about what I'll do, so I thought this time I'd try to reach out before I did anything.'

'Right.' She looked bored. 'Have you made specific plans, have you thought about exactly how you'd do it?'

I hate that question. Every time you admit to a medical professional that you're depressed or suicidal, they ask you if you've made 'specific plans'. Like it's a dinner reservation and they want to know if you're serious about turning up. I think the idea is that if you haven't made specific plans, you're not really going to go through with it. Which is bullshit. Let me tell you something: any person who feels suicidal enough that they go and talk to someone about it has made specific fucking plans. People reach out because they're told time and time again that that's what they should do. Then they get asked about 'specifics' in a way that always seems accusatory. Like if you had a plan, you would have just gone through with it and you wouldn't be here clogging up the ER.

'Yes,' I mumbled.

'What?' she said again. 'Speak *up*.'

I could barely get my voice above a whimper. Also, it's humiliating to have to tell someone who looks like they're itching to go to lunch some of the most private thoughts you've ever had.

'Um, pills. I was going to take pills.'

'What pills?'

'I don't know,' I said, tears welling in my eyes. 'Just whatever I could find.'

She was writing on my chart and not looking at me. She told me they were going to give me a letter to give to my psychiatrist, and send me home with some Valium. I started to panic.

'Wait, what? No. I need help. I need to stay here.'

'I think you just need a little something to calm you down, and as long as there's someone with you, there's no reason you can't go home. We'll have someone from mental health services call you in a few days to see how you're doing.'

I couldn't believe what I was hearing. Finally, for the first time ever, I had done what I was supposed to do – instead of taking the pills, I had reached out to someone who took me to the hospital. And now the hospital was sending me home. With more pills.

I mustered every bit of strength I had in my chaotic brain. 'No,' I said, as assertively as I could manage, considering I was wearing pyjamas at lunchtime. 'If you send me home, I will kill myself. I need to stay here.'

She sighed. 'Are you threatening to kill yourself unless we admit you?'

'Yes,' I said. 'I'm afraid of what I'll do if I go home.'

'You're afraid, or you'll actually do it?'

I couldn't believe I was playing this game of verbal chicken with someone I desperately needed help from.

'I'll actually do it,' I said.

'Fine,' she said before getting up and walking out of the room.

About an hour later, I was admitted into an emergency mental-health bed for an overnight stay. The next day, I was discharged. They didn't think I needed to be moved to the long-term facility because I 'hadn't *actually* attempted'.

I got in a taxi, went home, found every pill in the house and took them all. These weren't just headache tablets. This was everything. Everything in my flatmate's room. Everything in my room. Everything in the bathroom. Everything in the kitchen. My head felt like it was on fire. Then, nothing.

I woke up in the emergency room, tubes coming out of a million different places and my two best friends standing over me. 'Hey, crazy lady,' Tonz said, smiling. I loved that I had the kind of friends who would make inappropriate jokes while I was lying in a hospital bed. 'Bad day?' We all burst out laughing.

Apparently my sister had been worried when I was discharged earlier that day. She called my flatmate and my best friend Jacob, who found me unconscious on my flatmate's bed. They called an ambulance and I was rushed to hospital.

'Was it because of Luka?' Jacob asked me, when Tonz was in the bathroom.

'No. I don't know. Not really. I'm just sick of feeling like I want to die. It's all I think about. I can't turn my brain off. I really need help.'

'They're going to help you now, sweetie,' he said, looking determined. I fell back asleep.

In the morning, I was told I was going to be discharged with a note to my psychiatrist and some Valium. I was too defeated to fight back, but Jacob wasn't. You just try and argue with a bitchy gay – you'll never win. Jacob was not leaving that hospital unless he knew I was going to be admitted somewhere, long term. He demanded to see whoever was in charge, and a big Eastern European doctor with a very seedy moustache and a booming voice came to meet us about an hour later. I'm fairly certain he was some kind of epic porn star in his homeland.

'Leesin,' he said. 'We have mental ward here. But eet's not what she wants, trust me. These people are crazy. They feenger-paint in there. Do you want to just sit around feenger-painting?'

'Rosie is suicidal,' Jacob snapped. 'She has said that if she goes home, she will try to kill herself again. She doesn't give a fuck about being with people who finger-paint. She just needs help. I can't believe that she's reaching out and nobody is willing to help her. Surely there's a duty of care issue, if you send her home and she dies? In fact, I'd like to see you write it in the chart – "Rosie has said if we send her home she will kill herself." Write that down.'

The moustache porn doctor looked at me. 'Have you thought of speceefic plan?'

'Of course she's thought of a specific fucking plan,' Jacob said. 'Last night she took over a hundred pills. How's that for a plan? She needs help.'

'Fine,' the doc said, throwing his arms up in the air like he'd just lost at Bingo. 'We will admit her. I'm telling you, though, she will hate it.'

Jacob saved my life that day. If he hadn't been there, I would have given up and gone home, and I hate to think what I would have done. When up against Australia's shitty public mental-health system, never underestimate the power of having a very sassy gay man on your side. He was not going to stop until that possibly-once-a-porn-star doctor gave me a bed.

And what a bed it was. An ER nurse took me over to the separate mental hospital. It was about a five-minute walk away, fenced off with barbed wire. The doors were locked, and security checked us as we walked in. I was taken to the room that I would stay in for the next few weeks. Everything was suicide-proof. There was nowhere you could hang anything. The windows were made of two layers of glass, so that the blinds could sit between them and not be touched. There were no knobs on any of the drawers, cupboards or doors.

I sat on the tiny, single hospital bed for a while and took a long, deep breath. I was safe. I couldn't hurt myself here. For the first time in days, I started to feel calm.

I quietly ventured out to the main area to see what I had signed up for (and to possibly get in on that finger-painting, if it really was a thing). It was pretty grim. I'd describe the decor as 'suicide-proof nursing home chic'. There was a main common area, with a tiny TV. Next to that was the nurses' station and the kitchen, our only access to which was via a window that food came out of. The yard outside was basically just some grass and a table and chairs. It was surrounded by a very ominous looking, very high fence.

The toilets were … well, have you ever tried going to the toilet at a train station? Imagine that, but if the toilet was used exclusively by mentally ill people. In the first one I entered, I found shit smeared on the walls. The others all smelled like they'd recently had smeared shit cleaned from the walls.

Then there were the patients. I think the majority of them were homeless, and I actually saw one of them begging on George Street in Sydney a few years later. One man had just had some serious brain surgery, which had left him with a shaved head and a mammoth scar. With no clothes and no possessions, he had to walk around wearing hospital-issued pyjamas, and, thanks to the surgery, everything he did was in slow motion. I once timed him take over five minutes to lift his hand, scratch his face, then put his hand back down again. There were two pretty rough women who I think had been transferred there from some nightmarish rehab–prison hybrid. They were epic and horrifying, and if they weren't calling each other 'fuckin' cunts', they were looking for someone else to go after. One guy walked around with a tampon in his mouth, which I could never quite work out, although given how little I understood periods when I first got them, I'm surprised I had never tried that myself. Then, of course, there was PK, the man who insisted on walking around wearing nothing but his bedsheet as a toga.

I mostly kept to myself, except at mealtimes, which were terrifying. The dinner line was competitive, usually with the rough 'cunt' ladies leading the charge. It was like a school canteen but with sixty mentally ill adults hustling for a bigger portion of gravy. More than a few fights broke out in that line, probably because a lot of those people had been having to hustle for food for a very long time. I gladly took last position every night, even if it did mean I got the dodgy, overcooked end piece of lamb. I would rather eat dry meat than get stabbed with a fork.

I spent virtually my entire first week sleeping. Public mental-health care isn't exactly hands on: you are basically just plonked in a locked building to stop you from being harmful either to yourself, or to others. The plan to help you stops there. Every few days, I would see a psychiatrist for five minutes to make sure my medication was right, and that was it. The rest of the time I could watch the tiny TV, 'feenger-paint' or sit in the garden and watch the rough ladies yell 'cunt' at each other. That's about it. I preferred (partly out of terror, but mostly out of the need to be alone) to stay in my room. Where I slept and slept and slept and slept. A nurse would sometimes come in and wake me to give me a pill, then I would go back to sleep.

After that first week of sleep, my brain felt less chaotic. I started to stay up all night writing. Writing journals, writing letters to Luka that I would never send. Writing obsessively, page after page after page, trying to figure out exactly how I ended up in a mental ward at the age of twenty-four.

I thought a lot about why I had relied so much on Josh and Luka to get me through. I thought about the kind of person I had imagined I would be when I grew up. All those Oscars speeches I used to give in my room, all those incredible goals I was sure I was going to achieve. I had never pictured a man in any of that. Why had I now become so desperate to be loved that I tried to kill myself when I got dumped?

My writing sessions became very self-indulgent and existential. There was lots of staring out the window, sighing deeply and trying to collect my thoughts. I didn't keep any of those pages, but I'm sure I'd cringe if I looked at them now. It'd be like seeing a high-school book covered in pictures of Justin Timberlake back when his hair looked like two-minute noodles.

But all that feverish, stream-of-consciousness word vomit did lead me to realise one thing: there was a lot of trauma from my past that I needed to deal with, and nobody could deal with it but me. I needed to learn how to be alone. I needed to learn how to be my own hero.

I needed to stop waiting for a man to fly in and save me. I needed to stop pretending I was cool enough to take drugs in club bathrooms. I needed to roll up my sleeves, get to work on my mental health, and fly in and save my own damn self.

So, after three and a half weeks in the mental institution (most of which I spent trying not to get killed in the dinner line), I got out of bed, brushed my hair and told them I wanted to leave. I was going to conquer life! I was going to be like Winona Ryder at the end of that movie where she was nuts! I was going to be like any female character who finds herself at the end of any feel-good movie! I was going to get my damn shit together!

Then I spent the next three years hiding in my room, slowly gaining ninety kilos. Whoops.

You will watch your mum attempt suicide, and realise that she's the only one who understands you.

'Mummy?'

That was all I needed to say for her to snap into action. She booked me on a flight, using her very limited cash, to go and stay with her and her boyfriend in Dubbo. She explained things the way they needed to be explained to someone who's beyond hysterical.

'Rosanna. You need to get out of bed, darling. You need to pack a bag with some clothes. How long has it been since you've had a shower? Okay, you need to take a shower. Your plane leaves in four hours, so as soon as you're ready, call a taxi and go to the airport. But you can't leave any later than 2pm. When you get to Dubbo, get into a taxi and go to the address that I text you. It's going to be alright, darling. You can stay here as long as you need. What do you feel like for dinner? Rick wants to cook you something special.'

Just like when I was little, something about her calling me 'darling' calmed me down. My mum was always the last person I called for any kind of help with, well, anything. She was usually drunk or belligerent or just wanted to bitch about how one of my sisters had come over and eaten all her cabanossi. But after spending almost a month in a mental home, even I just needed my mummy.

And she understood that. She was the only person in my life who understood what I was going through. She understood what it felt like to have your brain insist that death is the only option, then to wake up the next day and have your brain laugh at you and say, 'Lol, jokes, you fucking nutcase.' She was the only person who understood that I was incapable of being an adult right then. That I could barely get out of bed, let alone book a flight. That even having to speak was like trying to force my body to lift an anvil. My mum knew that the dishes piled next to my bed couldn't be washed. She knew that I couldn't just 'go for a run'. She knew that my body was stone, and my mind was trying to eat itself.

My mum knew all of that because she'd been there herself, so many times. She knew that all I needed was to be taken care of, because that's all she'd wanted, so many times in the past. I needed my mummy, and my mummy finally felt like she was in a position to help.

I got on the plane to Dubbo.

She came to the door in her dressing gown, and pulled me

into a warm hug. I just wanted to suck every inch of her in and never let go. Apparently, when I was a baby, I would scream like a freaking banshee unless my mum was holding me. Nobody else could stop the crying. It probably had something to do with the fact that she took off when I was a few weeks old to party with her friends in Sydney, and would take off sporadically after that. I think I was a baby genius – even then I knew her presence was never going to be guaranteed, so when she was around, I insisted on being held, damn it.

And here I was again, twenty-four years old, getting the hug I desperately needed. Inside, Rick was already cooking me dinner, and the couch had been made up like a bed. Neither of them said anything about why I was there or where I'd been, they just welcomed me into their home and got to work looking after me. I flopped down on the couch and didn't get up again for my entire visit. They brought meals to my lap so I wouldn't have to move. My mum sat with me at night, and for the first time ever, we drank together. She sat with me at my laptop and listened as I read aloud the insufferable, long emails I was planning on sending Luka. She nodded earnestly and told me that they definitely weren't ridiculous or desperate when they absolutely were. We laughed about my sisters and watched TV together, and I snuggled into her shoulder while I fell asleep. We talked about how nobody understands what it feels like to have such pain and emptiness inside you that you can barely move or speak. We talked about how the brain in your head when you try to kill yourself is different from the brain in your head when you feel fine.

As I sat on that couch in Dubbo, eating roast chicken and cheesy potato bake and drinking cheap wine, I realised that I was so lucky to have a mother who understood what it felt like to be surrounded by darkness. As she took care of me and cleared my plates away and didn't complain that I hadn't showered once since I'd arrived, I realised that she was the only person in my life who really understood what it felt like to have no control over your brain. Just like when I was a baby, she was the only one who could comfort me now. She had failed me so many times before, but this week, this one week, she was there. And I couldn't help but think about how I had seen her in just as much pain a few years before, and I'd left her on her own. Just a few years earlier, when I was twenty-one and staying with Mum for a few weeks while I looked for a place of my own, I had stood by and watched through a window while she tried to kill herself.

Thirty seconds earlier and I would've walked straight past that window and not seen a thing. Thirty seconds earlier and I would've made it to my bedroom, never noticing that my mum was outside, trying to hang herself in the darkness.

But it wasn't thirty seconds earlier, and as soon as I saw her through that window, dragging a flimsy dining-room chair towards the front yard's only tree, I knew what she was doing.

And I had so been looking forward to watching *Letterman*.

I should have known that the evening was going to end in a particularly dramatic suicide attempt. After starting on her first bottle of wine mid-afternoon, by the time she finished her fourth at 7pm, she had already reached what I like to call her 'Dignified Royal' stage (a stage which involves far too much faux indignation for someone who only makes it to the toilet half the time).

It usually consisted of her sitting in the living room like a freshly crowned beauty queen, head held high and movements so fluid she was practically floating. Her cheap wine might as well be Cristal, her pleather couch a throne.

And there she would sit, taking grand, calculated sips from her mug of booze as she held her cigarette between her fingers like a sexy Disney villain.

'Rosanna,' she would say, in an accent that fell somewhere between her North Shore childhood and the cockroach-infested Liverpool rental where she currently sat. 'You, darling, have gained so much weight.' (No response.)

Or, 'How did I end up surrounded by so many fucking bogans?' (No response.)

Or, 'Why can't I fucking just send a fucking text to your fucking sister without the fucking thing being a fucking fuck?' (Sympathy shrug.)

I tried to keep her company for a while that night, but after a few hours of being picked apart by someone wearing green eyeliner and no pants, I decided it was probably in my best interest to bail out. I went to my room, turned on the TV and closed the door.

Nothing ever made me feel quite as safe as the sound of my bedroom door closing. TV and bed had been my refuge since childhood. As long as I had a door that closed and a show that made me laugh, I could pretend the mother in the next room was the perfect mix of Carol Brady and Lorelai Gilmore. I would have even settled for Roseanne, to be honest. I was pretty much just aiming for someone who didn't drunkenly listen to 'Bitter Sweet Symphony' on repeat (usually while snot-crying and eating olives out of a jar).

I'd had a TV friend in my room since I was four years old, and it was still keeping me company in my twenties. But on this particular night, just minutes before *Letterman* was about to start, my body betrayed me. I was forced to leave the confines of my free-to-air sanctuary. Basically, I needed to wee.

And it was on my way back to bed, as I walked past the upstairs window, that I spotted her dragging that bloody chair to that bloody tree.

Damn you, bladder.

I could tell she was thinking about how fabulously tragic the whole thing would look. She was wearing a pink satin dressing gown and nothing else – no doubt hoping that it would fall open dramatically as she hung, displaying the body that always got her through tough times.

The glow of the streetlights revealed that she had placed her frizzy curls into as elegant an up-do as she could manage, and she was definitely wearing more jewellery than she had been just hours earlier.

I stood silently at the window and watched as she positioned the chair under the tree. I was surprised to see she'd had the forethought to take rope, although I had no clue where she'd got it. I'd like to say she'd been on a morbid version of one of her shoplifting sprees, but considering the lack of planning that had most likely gone into this, I assumed tonight's hardware probably came from a store called the Neighbour's Clothesline.

She hoisted her mystery rope over the sturdiest-looking branch the tree had to offer, and carefully climbed up on the chair (as best as a person who's been drinking for nine hours can). Her dressing gown slipped open – perhaps a little too early for her dramatic reveal, but impromptu performances like this rarely went to plan.

She put the makeshift noose around her neck. She tightened it.

I knew I should be moving by now. But my feet were frozen to the floor, my eyes fixated on her face.

What if I just let it happen this time? What if I pretended it was thirty seconds earlier? What if I had never seen anything through that window, and I was already sitting in bed watching Letterman bounce jokes off Paul Shaffer? Nobody knew I was standing there. Nobody knew I was watching. Nobody knew that I left my room to wee. That thirty seconds was my clay to mould.

She was struggling with the chair now, trying to tip it over. She couldn't use her hands, and the rope was too short to readjust, so she just ended up rocking her whole body from side to side, trying to build up enough momentum to get the bloody thing to move.

And just as I was thinking that attempted suicide, along with coughing and vomiting, was probably one of the more unattractive things a person could do while naked, the chair tipped over.

She hung from the tree, gown open, feet shaking. And I didn't move. I just stood there, watching.

I just stood there.

I thought back to the time, years before, when I was just a kid, and I sat with her on the side of the road, desperately trying to think of the right response to, 'But, Rosie, I just want to die.'

I told her that her daughters needed her. That she needed to see us grow up. I told her I was going to write books and win an Oscar and become a millionaire and buy her a house and then she'd never have to worry about anything again. I told her I would take care of her, but I was only nine, so she needed to wait just a little longer.

I told her I was cold and wanted to go inside.

I thought back to the time I found her in a random park in the middle of the night, a slit in her left wrist so deep I was actually a little impressed she had managed it with such a flimsy kitchen knife. She sat on the grass quietly, staring blankly ahead as I tried to hold the gash together with a tea towel. I walked her home and put her to bed, then spent the entire night trying not to fall asleep so the grip I had on her wrist wouldn't loosen.

'Move, Rosie. *Move.*' I silently willed my body to leap into action, but it remained frozen in front of the window. It felt heavy. Tired. The glow of the TV was luring me to my room, and the idea of rest seemed too good to pass up. Rest for her. Rest for me. Rest, finally, for all of us.

I could pretend I'd walked past that window thirty seconds earlier. And I could just let it happen.

My mind was grappling with the complexities of a decision I should not have been attempting to make while wearing Hello Kitty pyjamas. But before I could make a choice, before I could decide whether I wanted those thirty seconds to exist or not, it happened.

The branch broke. The fucking branch broke. My mum fell to the ground, gasping for breath and ruining her frizzy up-do.

The decision had been made for me.

I watched as she slowly rose to her feet and (in what I considered an odd moment to suddenly feel modest) closed her dressing gown. She took the rope from around her neck and dropped it on the grass. Then she just walked back inside.

And that was it.

I heard the downstairs TV switch on, and the unmistakable clink of a wine bottle hitting a glass. I took one final look at the branch lying on the front lawn, before heading into my room and closing the door.

Thirty seconds earlier, and I would have missed the whole thing.

Her feet were only off the ground for a fleeting moment, but that branch breaking meant I never got to make my own decision. Was I just about to move? Was I just about to snap into action? Was I just about to run to her aid, like I had so many times before?

That branch breaking means I'll never truly know if I would have saved my mother's life that night.

Thirty seconds earlier, and I wouldn't have to spend the rest of my life wondering if I'm the kind of person who would just watch her mother die.

And as I sat on that couch in Dubbo a few years later, desperately clinging to every ounce of comfort she was giving me, I felt so guilty knowing that once I had given her none. Even though I knew that her comfort wouldn't last, and that once I got home it wouldn't be long before the drunken, abusive phone calls would start up again. But she had given me this one week. She knew she was the only one who understood, and she flew me out to her couch in Dubbo and fed me and tucked me in and stroked my hair and called me darling.

She gave me what I needed that week, and if the branch hadn't broken, I'd have been all alone. Just like she was the night I watched her nearly die.

You will gain ninety kilos, and it will be the best thing that has ever happened to you.

I officially knew my weight had gotten out of control when I realised I could no longer wipe my own arse.

I was so big that my arm was not physically long enough to reach under my belly and wipe the area behind my vagina otherwise known as the butt hole. For a while, I had solved the problem by hoisting one foot up on the toilet seat – that gave me a little wiggle room to reach down. But, eventually, even that wasn't enough. I had actually reached the stage where if I needed to poo, I would have to take a shower afterwards.

And I'd never had a more healthy sense of self-worth in my entire life. I couldn't wipe my own arse, and I loved myself more than I ever had.

After strutting out of the mental institution with my head held high, I had a minor setback and spent a week crying on my mum's couch. Then I had another minor setback, and barely left my bedroom for three years. My bad. I somehow, miraculously, managed to finish university and walk away with a degree in creative writing, then I got a job in a call centre so I would never have to see anyone, and that became my life.

Go to work, answer phones (and by 'answer phones', I mean read the paper and hang up on people as soon as the call gets too difficult), go home, eat myself into oblivion, throw up, watch TV, go to sleep. That was all I did for three years after that mental ward gave me 'a new lease on life'.

Don't get me wrong, I had learned a lot about myself during the time I spent self-reflecting there (sighing and staring wistfully out of windows can actually be helpful). I'd also continued with weekly therapy, working really fucking hard to understand my fear of abandonment and PTSD symptoms. Mentally, I had reached a profound place. My panic attacks had mostly subsided, my anxiety was at an all-time low, and I wasn't particularly depressed (unless, of course, the internet was out and I couldn't download *30 Rock*). I spent those three years learning how to be my own saviour, how to feel comfortable being single and how to be mentally healthy. But I was terrified to put any of these lessons into action.

I felt like my life until that point had been one giant clusterfuck after another, and if I could just stay in my room and not rock the boat, then nothing could go wrong. I completely took myself out of the game, because you can't lose if you don't play.

The weight gain began pretty much straight after leaving hospital. My disordered eating and messed-up attitude towards food had started back with that 'I'm pretending to be worried about nutrition, but really you're just getting fat' talk in drama school in 2006. It was now 2013, and I'd been on a cycle of binging and purging and starving that entire time. I'd spend three days eating only apples, then I'd be so starving that I'd stuff myself to the point of exploding and vomit everywhere. Whenever I was depressed, I'd buy ice-cream with Ice Magic, and I wouldn't mess around – I'd eat an entire litre of vanilla with three bottles of topping. Then I'd spew in the empty container and hide it under my bed. There were times when I had vomit hidden in secret places all over my room. Eventually, I'd screwed around with my body so badly that I developed hypothyroidism and completely fucked up my metabolism, which meant weight was easy to put on and very difficult to take off. The kilos starting piling on at a scary rate. Even with the purging, which had kept me in the 'chubby but still kind of attractive' safe zone in the past, I was just getting bigger and bigger.

Before I knew it, I had gained ninety kilos, and that was the perfect excuse to never leave my room again. I kept promising myself that I would start living my life the way I had planned three years earlier just as soon as I 'got my old body back'. Being fat was my new shield against the world.

And trust me, when you're fat, you need a shield. I was shocked by how differently I was treated as an obese person. People treat you as if you're subhuman. Particularly if you're a woman, since a woman's entire worth is almost always primarily based on her appearance. My very presence on earth seemed to offend people, particularly men. That I had the audacity to venture out in public as a fat woman really infuriated them. I was yelled at as I walked down the street ('fat bitch' being the most common). I was abused for taking up too much space on the bus. I was laughed at whenever I ate in public. Romantic attention was a thing of the past.

I felt so stupid that I had never realised my looks played such a huge role in what people valued about me, and once they were gone, I began to seriously question whether I had anything to offer.

Then I read a crappy article on the internet. I can't even remember what it was about to be honest, probably '27 reasons why brunette Gen Y's should get married in winter' or some bullshit. And it made a bell go off in my brain. I read it over and over, finding it so hard to believe that it had ever been published. Then I just thought, 'You know what, I can write a million times better than that. How come I'm not published on the internet?' Then I remembered, 'Oh, that's right, because your life revolves around waiting to stream your favourite TV shows and what take-out you're going to have for dinner.'

So, on a whim that afternoon, I wrote a piece for the internet. I made it purposefully provocative so that it had a chance of being published. I created a basic WordPress blog, registered the domain name 'rosiewaterland.com' and posted it. Then I sent the link to Australia's top women's website, Mamamia, and asked if they'd be interested in publishing it. I had no idea if you could just email editors like that, since I had studied creative writing at uni and not journalism, which basically meant I had no vocational skills whatsoever. I'd once handed in an assignment that listed fifty synonyms for the word vagina, said it was about minimalism and feminism, and got a high distinction. That's what my entire uni course was like – laughing my head off the night before an assignment was due, drinking half a box of wine, scribbling something onto the page and thinking, 'How the fuck am I getting a degree out of this?' Then I'd just shrug my shoulders and finish the rest of the wine. So, unlike the journalism graduates, I had very little clue about what approaching editors or publications entailed, or even how to write a proper column. I just went with my gut.

That afternoon, I got an email reply from Mamamia's then managing editor, Jamila Rizvi. They loved my piece and wanted to publish it. I started to cry. I couldn't believe that I had barely dipped my toe in the water of life, and already something positive had happened. This is the very first piece of mine that was ever professionally published:

I once had a boyfriend who told me he thought I'd be less of a woman if I didn't want to give birth 'naturally'.

Of course, this was the same boyfriend who literally threw up a little the one time in our two-year relationship I dared to fart in his presence, so in hindsight he had some serious issues when it came to his ideas about women.

I was telling him one day about my sister's experience with childbirth. She went through such excruciating pain during her labour that she still maintains with all seriousness that if someone hadn't been in the room with her the entire time she would have jumped out the third-storey window.

I then went on to tell him that when I eventually get pregnant, I have a genius c-section/tummy-tuck plan that involves waking up with a gunk-free baby in a fluffy blanket sleeping peacefully next to me. Brilliant, no? I waited for him to applaud my practical approach to childbirth. He would never want the woman he loves to be in so much physical pain that she would jump out a third-storey window. Right?

Unfortunately, the applause never came. Instead, there was some nervous laughter, followed by something along the lines of, 'but obviously you want to go through it, right? I mean, jokes aside Rosie, it's important for a woman to experience birth the proper way ...'

He laughed, thinking I was kidding. I laughed, thinking he was kidding. Then as it slowly dawned on each of us that the other was dead serious, we managed to say an awkward 'wait … what?' in unison before a very tense silence took hold of the room.

Needless to say, we're no longer together. But it did plant a nagging seed in my mind that I still find difficult to get rid of. Am I the only one? The only woman with no qualms about planning a c-section in order to avoid pain and keep my lady parts intact.

Is anyone else just not interested in pushing a baby out of their vagina?

My ex-boyfriend isn't alone; I've had both male and female friends react strongly when I've told them my future c-section plan. To me (well, for me), it's an absolute no-brainer. We no longer expect some poor chump to bite down on a leather strap and be brave while we amputate one of his limbs — so why do we still expect a woman to go through even worse agony to have a child? The hyperbolic rants I go on when I knock my elbow should be some indication of how I handle pain. Not well, evidently. I can't imagine myself in the throes of baby delivering.

I think my birthing anxiety stems back to a book my mum left on the bottom shelf when I was in kindergarten. It was for expectant mothers and had lots of extremely graphic pictures of women with '80s haircuts and twisted faces pushing out babies. And did I mention graphic?

All I knew was this thing I currently identified as a 'wee-wee' was eventually going to be ripped apart while I lay with my legs in the air on some bed of excruciating pain.

I'm guessing that's the reason I've never associated childbirth as some kind of romantic female rite of passage. But don't get me wrong; I absolutely respect the women who do want to give birth the old-fashioned way. In fact, I think any woman who gives it a go deserves some kind of prize (I know the baby should be prize enough and blah blah blah, but I'm thinking more an ASOS voucher).

In fact, any woman who gives birth in any kind of way deserves a prize (let's not forget the residual pain of a c-section that many women love to remind me about); even those lottery-winning ladies of legend who orgasm during childbirth had to carry the thing around for nine months.

I guess the trick lies in finding a partner who has the same push values as you do. Because no matter what way a woman decides to remove an entire person from her body, that decision should be accepted with the utmost respect and enthusiasm (and absolutely no comment on your perceived notion of her level of 'womanhood').

I may not get the appeal of pushing; you may not get the appeal of having a massive gash healing across one's stomach

for months just to avoid labour. Does it matter? Everyone has
a thousand sleepless nights and nappies to look forward to, so
what's the difference really?

I cringe a little reading it now, but all I really wanted was to make people laugh. Actually, because it was the internet and the internet is a cesspool of bored hatred trolls, it ended up making most people really angry, all of whom decided to send me an email. Which I fucking loved.

After that article, I sent Mamamia another, and another, and another. I was publishing on my blog quite frequently, and it was starting to build up a little following of its own. (No doubt helped by my friend Tonz tweeting things like '@JustinBieber and @SelenaGomez BABY? This source says so ...' followed by a link to my blog. I may have got a lot of clicks from disappointed tweens, but at least they were clicks.)

I loved being published. Every time I made people laugh, it was like fuel for my soul. I started to feel a little more confident, like maybe I could very cautiously think about putting myself back in the game, so I asked Jamila if I could come to Mamamia and do an internship.

I was nervous about my weight, but I wanted to write and Mamamia was giving me a chance, so when Jamila agreed, I put on my most stylish black muu-muu and went for it.

The only thing I remember about my first day is meeting Mia Freedman, the founder and publisher of Mamamia. She edited *Dolly* when I was reading *Dolly*, and then *Cosmo* when I was reading *Cosmo*. I had been looking at her face in magazines since I was a kid. And when she walked into the office and saw me, she knew my damn name. 'Rosie!' she exclaimed, arms opened wide for a hug. 'I'm such a huge fan! I'm so glad you're here interning!' I was a little taken aback. Not only was Mia Freedman saying words to me that sounded a lot like my name, she had just given me a freaking hug.

We clicked straight away. She would single me out in editorial meetings, giving me way more to write than the other interns. We had inside jokes within about thirty seconds of knowing each other. After two weeks, I was offered a job as an editorial assistant. A few months later, I was promoted to editor of an entire section of the website.

I had taken a minor chance, and it had paid off in a major way. I went from hiding in my room, working in a call centre and watching TV, to being an editor at the biggest women's website in the country. I went from Jamila literally having to drag me to drinks after work, to organising entire office social functions myself. I was starting to feel more like myself than I had in years. I was laughing again, and I was making other people laugh, which I loved more than anything.

But still, the weight. I couldn't get the weight out of my mind. I was achieving so much, and I still felt worthless because of my damn weight. So, one night I wrote an article saying how depressed I was about how I looked. I admitted that I was fat, and included photos. I know the word 'admitted' sounds strange, because everybody who sees you obviously knows that you are. But I honestly thought that if I saw as few people as possible (and covered up around the ones I couldn't avoid), nobody would ever have to know. Everybody would still think of me as 'the old Rosie', 'the thin Rosie', and in the meantime, I would lose the weight and they would be none the wiser.

So writing a piece about my obesity and the reality of how it had affected my life was a massively revealing moment for me. Having it published on Mamamia sealed the deal. I was fat. And now everybody knew.

I thought I would be mortified. After all, this was the exact humiliating situation I had been trying to avoid. But my world didn't collapse. The majority of people weren't horrible.

Old friends reached out to me and didn't mention my weight at all. (I'm not sure what I was expecting. Probably something like: 'Dear Rosie, you're massive now. Gross. Regards, your old friend Jimmy.')

Writing that piece and receiving such a positive reaction was like dipping my toe even further into the water of life. Inch by inch, I was stepping more into the game. I admitted I was fat and my world didn't implode. People still read my writing, still thought I had value and something to offer regardless of my size. That was a big deal for me.

I started to have crazy thoughts, like maybe I deserved to be loved and valued in spite of my weight. I decided to make *loving myself* the goal, rather than weight loss. I began seeing an eating disorder specialist, who focussed on health and not size. And at that point in time, 'health' was getting me to a place where I felt good about myself, at any size. 'Health' for me was building my self-esteem, which for years had been non-existent.

These were difficult concepts to comprehend, since women basically have it drummed into them from birth that their looks are the most important thing about them. But recalibrating what I considered worthy changed my life. I was a survivor, damn it. I had made it through a crazy childhood, worked incredibly hard to fix my mental health, got a degree and was now a popular writer at a major website. I began to write a lot about self-acceptance and self-love, and the importance of teaching girls that they are more than their appearance. I was finally kicking life's arse! Who gave a fuck if I was fat?

I had that attitude, and was proud of myself for getting there, until the day I realised I couldn't wipe my own arse. I had finally come to love myself, but nobody wants to walk around with poo residue between their bum cheeks.

I'd also begun to notice that, working in media particularly, my looks were something that seemed to matter. Despite being surrounded by incredible women at Mamamia who loved me and supported me and gently coaxed me out of a very dark place in my life, despite my rising success, despite having what was probably the healthiest attitude towards my body and food in years, I couldn't control what other people valued in me. And a lot of people only saw fat when they looked at me, which fucking sucked. It seemed so unfair, that after coming so far in my quest for self-acceptance, after jumping so many hurdles in an effort to love and value myself for the right reasons, there was still one hurdle that I would never have any control over: I could never control what other people valued about me.

Also, there was the whole bum-wiping thing.

So, reluctantly, I organised to get weight-loss surgery. I was so ashamed at the time, and so pissed off because I felt like I was doing it more for other people than for me. And even though a bunch of health reasons had contributed to my weight gain and made it difficult for me to lose weight naturally, I still felt like I was betraying people. I had gone through such an attitude transformation, and I had encouraged so many Mamamia readers to do the same. I waxed lyrical about 'loving yourself no matter what', and now I was sneaking off for five weeks to have eighty percent of my stomach removed. But whenever I felt like I was doing the wrong thing, or that I was betraying the self-love sisterhood, I reminded myself of one important fact: 'Rosie. You can't wipe your own goddamn arse.'

When I woke up from the surgery, I kept insisting my name was Oprah and demanding to know if I 'was skinny yet'. I spent a week in hospital in a lot of pain, followed by three weeks at home (paid, because that's the kind of brilliant boss Mia Freedman is), drinking nothing but clear liquids. It was hell. I cannot describe the torture that is desperately wanting to eat something, but physically not being able to. I mostly just sat in bed, feeling very sorry for myself, watching TV and dreaming about the steak that I would never eat again.

The next year was just as hard. It took months before I could even think about eating solid food, and even then, the tiniest amount would make me vomit. I felt sick all the time. I was scared to eat in restaurants, in case I suddenly needed to spew. There was also a lot of emotional fallout that came with throwing up being such a regular part of my life again, since I had worked so hard to stop doing that voluntarily. But I lost a ridiculous amount of weight, and will probably continue to do so. I don't know exactly how much I've dropped, because I refuse to weigh myself. I don't want that number to mean anything to me ever again.

I'm relieved, though, that I really took the time to learn how to love myself, because my body is definitely ... *different* now. Losing weight quickly does things to you. Freaky things. I'm certainly a lot thinner, but everything is squishy and stretched and droopy now. My boobs look like two sandwich bags that have been half-filled with custard. My stomach is covered in stretch marks and hangs down like a sad roly-poly dog. I can take the skin under my arms and stretch it out like play dough. And let's not even get into my droopy FUPA situation.

But I honestly don't care. Coming to work at Mamamia gave me the confidence to learn that my weight and my body aren't the most important things about me. Gaining ninety kilos was the experience that taught me to love myself. To *really* love myself. And that is probably one of the greatest things that's ever happened to me. Would it be nice to look like Gemma Ward? Sure. But I have an incredible brain and the ability to write, and I make people laugh pretty much every day. I wouldn't give that up for anything. Those are the things I've learned to value. Also, I'm going to have the rare privilege of ageing without freaking the fuck out. I've already lived most people's aesthetic worst nightmare – getting old is going to be a walk in the park for me.

And, I really can't stress this one enough: it is such a fucking relief to be able to wipe my own arse.

Someone will play Jenga with your face and their penis, and you will consider it a sexual revolution.

I once scared a penis back inside itself.

I was trying so freaking hard to impress a guy with my brilliant sexual prowess that it had the opposite effect. One second his peen was there, and as soon as I tried to be sexy, it was gone. Not unlike when a turtle sees a predator and shoves his head inside the shell for safety.

I actually made a dick feel like it needed safety.

I was trying one of those *Cosmo* sex tips, and let me just put this out there right now: those tips *do not fucking work*. But of course, I was young, and because I was getting my sex advice from women's magazines, I was yet to realise that sex had anything to do with my pleasure. For a really long time, as far as I was concerned, if the guy blew his load and made some kind of audible sound that indicated pleasure, then I had done my job and the sex was over. I could secretly get myself off later in the bathroom – the sex part was all about him.

It was that sad and ridiculous attitude that got me caught up in many unfortunate situations, all while trying desperately to please a man. The first of which was the pretty pink penis bow, which scared the penis back inside itself.

I was young – I think about a year out of high school. I was still with Josh, my lovely first boyfriend, and since we had been each other's first, we'd done the thing all young people do when they realise their private parts connect – we tried to make our private parts connect in all the crazy ways we could think of. But, as is the way with all relationships, the initial passion, which results in you having sex anywhere there happens to be a horizontal surface, eventually wears off. And that's when Josh and I found ourselves in a bit of a boring sexual routine.

So I did what any young, misguided woman was supposed to do when a sex problem was getting her down: I consulted a women's mag. I was immediately informed that I was in what's called a 'sexual rut'.

I was also told that this was possibly the worst thing that could happen to any young lady who would like to hold on to her man. 'Shit,' I thought. 'I'm a young lady and I'd like to hold on to my man.' I actually hadn't realised my man was trying to get away from me until the magazine told me so, but I suddenly became very desperate to make sure I kept him in my clutches.

I should point out here that I know all this is ridiculous. I know this *now*.

But back then, I had no clue what was what. It was my first proper relationship; I had no idea that the initial passion grows into something deeper and blah, blah, love, blah. All I knew was that the sex had gone from fifteen times a week to five and this magazine was telling me that was my fault. But, thank the *Cosmo* heavens, they also had a solution.

I can't remember exactly what the article was called, but I'm sure it included the words 'hot' and 'sizzling' and lots of exclamation marks. And probably the word 'blow' in capital letters.

There was a bunch of very complicated tips I could use to keep my man. I picked the one I thought would be the cheapest (I was a student) and the simplest (I was terrified). Basically, I was instructed to find a bow, like the one you put on top of a gift box. Then, I was meant to tell my man I had a 'present' for him. My job was to get him excited by sending him texts all day reminding him of the aforementioned present. Then, when he was sufficiently excited, I had to tell him that it was time for his present, but first he had to lay down on the bed and close his eyes ...

Then I was supposed to give him an erection (no explanation provided – just get him there). Once he was sufficiently aroused, I was to take the bow and put it on his penis. At that moment, he was finally allowed to open his eyes, and he would immediately look down to see his penis gussied up like a present.

That was when I was supposed to say something along the lines of 'Surprise! Your present is a *sizzling hot* head job that will *blow* your mind!' I can't quite believe the level of naïveté that convinced me this would be sexy, but I went for it.

I texted Josh all morning about the 'amazing' present I had for him. But by the afternoon, I had lost interest in the game, so the texts trailed off and I forgot about the whole thing. So when he got to my house and demanded his amazing gift, I was a little thrown. 'Oh … yeah,' I thought. 'That thing I was going to do …' I told him to close his eyes.

'Oh!' he said, clearly excited now. 'Is this a sexy present?'

'Yep,' I said, rummaging through my craft box, looking for a bow. I hadn't planned this very well. Not only did I not have a bow handy, I was also wearing flannelette pyjamas. And I was tired and in no mood for giving a head job.

Actually, I was never in the mood to give a head job, really. Still not. Can we all just take a moment to acknowledge that giving head is the fucking worst? (It's okay – you're reading this in your mind right now so nobody has to know that you agree.)

I understand, as unjust as it is, that most ladies (and I suspect a lot of guys) feel like they can't admit to having unpleasant feelings about sausage-shaped chunks of rigid flesh being shoved repeatedly into their mouths.

There seems to be a general feeling that one must pretend to enjoy performing oral sex or risk a life of loneliness, listening to Taylor Swift while getting into Twitter fights with people about Jennifer Aniston's romantic future.

I get it. There's pressure to conform. But this is a safe place, and I think we all just need to admit that eating penis isn't enjoyable.

Don't get me wrong – I totally accept that giving lady-head would be just as unpleasant an experience. I can't imagine that having to swim through my pube garden would be easy by any means. But it's all about doing something nice for someone else and taking one for the team. So while I understand that enjoyment can come from doing something that your partner enjoys, that doesn't mean *you* have to actually enjoy the sweaty-balled, sperm-inducing act itself.

Let's break it down, shall we?

It usually begins with a make-out session that is rudely interrupted by the not-so-subtle pushing down of the head. That is the penis owner's code for: 'I would like an orgasm that requires no physical exertion on my part. Thanks in advance.'

If you accept your fate and agree to be a selfless blow-job hero, you then have to pull off the dude's undies and untangle his sweaty bulge from his hairy balls (one of which always needs to be peeled off the inside of his leg) and unfurl them like one of those wrinkly puppies stretching out in the sun.

All the sweat that has been collecting in between his pubes from hours locked inside his penis-oven now glistens on your hands, which you try to politely wipe on the bed/carpet/your own pants without him seeing. Because romance/magic/don't ever dare ruin the moment etc.

After some obligatory kissing of the general area, you eventually realise that you've put off the inevitable long enough – you must take the actual penis into your mouth. You can only cup sweaty balls and kiss the safe zone between the belly button and the pubes for so long. You must get down to business.

(Also, let's take a brief moment here to acknowledge that even the concept of putting something in your mouth that was probably shooting out urine just minutes ago is straight-up gross.)

It's important you try to get comfortable now, as there will be some sustained physical effort on your part. The key word being 'try', as comfort for a person giving a head job is generally regarded as an urban myth. You'll either get a dead leg from being on your knees, or an aching arm from lying on your side and trying to hold up the top half of your body with one elbow.

Highest possible comfort level (that is, not very) attained, you must then 'ease' into proceedings, as just shoving the whole thing into your mouth and letting it sit there like a docked boat until it explodes is, unfortunately, considered poor form.

You must try to coat the whole shaft in your (sexy, make sure it's sexy) saliva to ensure adequate lubrication for your hands (usually still covered in glistening ball sweat), which will shoulder some of the workload while you avoid the inevitable for as long as possible: the attempted deep-throat.

It is a truth universally acknowledged, that a single man in possession of a penis must be in want of an individual to deep-throat it. And no matter how many times he has tried and failed, he will grab the back of your head mid-blow-job and try to push it as far forward as he can.

Men tend to forget the concept of head ownership during sexy-times; they assume that if their penis is currently attached to someone's head, it indicates ownership of that head. *It does not indicate ownership of that head.* The person who owns the head knows how far it can go in, okay?

It's at this point that you are usually expected to begin 'sexy moaning'. This involves ignoring the fact you currently have a penis trying to poke the top of your left lung, so that you may concentrate on making the relevant human sounds that indicate sexual pleasure.

It is also, though not always, expected that you make sexy eye contact with very sexual eyes. It should also be noted here that looking sexy with your gaping mouth stretched around a penis is impossible – no amount of sexy eyes is going to fix that.

It's been said that a very rare and select group of women look attractive while crying – I suspect those are the only women who look attractive with a dick in their mouths.

Here's where things start to speed up. At this point you are basically like one of those perpetual-motion chicken toys that drinks the coloured water, except on steroids. All pretence of hand involvement is forgotten. This part is all about you trying not to gag as your head moves back and forth at an exponential rate. You must resist the urge to switch whatever leg/elbow/hand/toe you are leaning on, or the rhythm will be interrupted and you may end up having to go even longer.

The lips you have wrapped around your teeth to protect his precious manhood are starting to feel the pressure. All you can think about is how much easier this would be if you were fitter. You desperately need a glass of water.

Then …

He finishes. Which is just a nice way of saying that he explodes one billion little wriggly sperm into your mouth, which immediately begin gasping for air, racing towards an egg they'll never find.

Grouped together, sperm have the consistency of warm snot and the taste of broken dreams. And it doesn't matter whether you spit or swallow; some of them will definitely end up wedged in sad little sperm graveyards between your teeth.

So, that's it. Not unbearable, but certainly not pleasant. I'm not saying that I never do it. I'm just saying that I hate it. And I know, I *know*, I'm not the only one.

Because giving head is the worst. (Now please excuse me while I go and watch any chance I had to find a man slowly fade away.)

Um, where were we? Ah yes, finding a bow to put on my boyfriend's dick so *Cosmo* wouldn't consider me a failure.

Despite my reservations about blow jobs, by this point I had teased him enough that he was sufficiently into the whole thing, and expectations were high. Not to mention, *Cosmo* was telling me that if I didn't do something drastic in the bedroom, our relationship would be over and I would (gasp!) not be married by the time I was thirty. So I decided to improvise.

I found a pastel-pink piece of ribbon in my craft box. It seemed long enough that I would be able to do something sexy-ish with it.

'Okaaaaay,' I said, trying out the sexiest voice I could muster (I just assumed elongating words made them sexy). 'It's time for your preseeeent!' The poor guy was lying there with his eyes closed and his pants down, clearly expecting the most amazing sexual experience of his life.

I approached his penis with the ribbon. The most logical way to do it seemed to be to tie the ribbon around the shaft like a shoelace. I tried that, but it just looked a bit … shit. And the pastel-pink colour wasn't helping.

I spent the next couple of minutes trying to tie it a bunch of different ways, but no matter what I did, the ribbon just looked like it belonged around the neck of an itty-bitty puppy, tied in a dainty bow.

'What's going on?' my boyfriend asked, clearly confused.

'Shut up,' I said in my sexiest voice. 'I'm being seeeexy.'

Eventually, the ribbon was as good as it was going to get.

'Okay,' I said. 'Open your eyes!'

He looked down at his penis.

'What the fuck is that?' he asked.

'What?' I said. 'It's sexy. I'm giving you a sexy blow-job present.'

'But why is my penis covered in a pretty hair ribbon?' He was perplexed.

'Um … because … I wrapped it like a present? Because sexy?'

We both looked down at his penis again. I appeared to have shocked it back into itself. So now the pastel-pink ribbon was tied in a pretty bow around a soft-looking pile of skin. I felt like I should name it Petunia and take it to high tea.

We did not have sex that night.

And if the pretty pink penis bow was the beginning of my quest to impress men sexually, the Tinder date was the end. This was the night I realised it was time for a sexual revolution. I was twenty-eight, it had been ten years since the failed *Cosmo* sex tip, and it was finally time for me to stop letting sex be all about the guy.

The Tinder date was … actually, I'm not entirely sure what it was. Let's just say I ended the night slightly confused, but with all my suspicions about this 'exciting' Tinder thing confirmed. Like a kid who sees Santa without his beard on leaving a shopping centre in his Toyota Corolla.

To be totally upfront, this (one and only) Tinder date was actually also the first date I'd ever been on. Yeah, I was twenty-eight, and it wasn't my first romantic entanglement by any means. I'd been in two long-term relationships and had a steady stream of hook-ups and messy one-nighters outside of those. But I'd never actually done the part that comes *between* those two extremes.

The two boys I'd loved were my friends before anything else, and I'm pretty sure I tricked them both into pairing up with me before they realised what was happening. 'Oh?' I would say, when they asked about that bikini wax I'd said I got religiously when we were still friends. 'I said that, did I?' Then I'd hike up my flannelette pyjama pants and spend the night farting in my sleep.

So, relationships, I had done. Hook-ups, I had done. But a date? An actual, awkward, 'We both know what's going on but we're not going to say it' date? Never. Something about that has always felt … *off* to me. Why admit that you like someone and that you're hoping they like you back? Why would you ever give anyone that kind of power? *What kind of sick masochist would enjoy that?*

Not me. I was perfectly happy to continue on with my plan of being alone, waiting for the day a smart, funny man would read something brilliant I had written, fall instantly in love, and ironically wait outside the Mamamia offices with a boom box playing that song from that movie I'm not old enough to remember.

But then came Tinder. And after a drunken, embarrassingly giggly cliché of a night with my girlfriends, I promised to sign up for twenty-four hours. And even though I had ample warning from the moment I started playing, I somehow didn't realise Tinder was essentially just an online pimp until about hour twenty-three.

In hour one, I was still finding my bearings. I quickly discovered that, in Tinderland, anybody not asking you about the possibility of inserting a range of objects into your vagina instantly seems like a gentleman. That's how I ended up chatting to someone who enquired about my nipple and its current state of erection. 'At least he's keeping it above the waist' is actually a thought that went through my brain.

I should have known my standards had dropped dramatically when I started enjoying talking to Nipple Guy. It had only been forty-five minutes and Tinder had already broken my brain.

Nipple Guy messaged me several times the next morning, and, encouragingly, all of it was civil and nipple-talk-free. He asked if I wanted to meet up that night, and with my 24-hour time-limit in mind, I said yes.

At twenty-eight years of age, I had successfully set up my very first date.

Now, as hard as I've tried to be cool since the moment I shat my pants and pretended I hadn't so I could hang out with my big sister's friends, I'm not cool in even the most generous interpretation of the word. So while other people would have wondered if sex was on the table, that thought didn't even cross my mind. When he suggested I go to his house to have a few drinks and watch some TV, I thought, 'Yes! Amazing! Someone else who hates going out on Saturday night!' When he suggested I come at 9pm, I thought, 'Yes! Amazing! Now I have time to drink wine in the shower before I leave!'

And that's how I found myself, at 9pm on a Saturday night, having very average intercourse with a dude who had charmed me by being polite enough not to send me a dick pic. And yes – intercourse is the most appropriate word I can think of in this circumstance.

Things started off fine. There was chatting and drinks. I knew immediately that it wasn't a love-connection, but I was determined to commit to the whole experience. (I'm a writer! I must live life! etc etc etc.) I somehow turned the conversation to feminism, which he very politely endured, considering he was probably confused as to why I wasn't rubbing my nipple on his ball sack yet.

Then (and in hindsight, I understand that this is the point I probably should have realised he was really, really hoping for sex), he stood up, cracked a joke about 'pants-free Saturdays', and proceeded to take off his jeans. He then sat back down on the couch and kept chatting, like it was totally normal that he was now wearing only underpants.

I didn't quite know how to respond.

'I'm not taking my pants off,' I blurted out.

'That's fine,' he said, before continuing on with his very valid point about sexism in the workplace.

Somehow, I still didn't realise that he was hoping for sex. I didn't even pick up on it when he suggested watching a movie in his bedroom. 'I love watching movies in my bedroom!' I thought. 'Me and this guy have so much in common! Dating is fun!'

So there we were, sitting on his bed, watching TV. I felt a little strange about the no-pants situation, but who was I to dictate how he dressed in his own home? I figured I must just be one of those people who is so adept at putting others at ease, he just felt like he could relax around me. 'Well done, Rosie,' I thought. 'You are so fucking personable.'

But then, just as I was giving myself a mental pat on the back for being so incredible at getting along with strangers, Nipple Guy took things up a notch.

Without taking his eyes off the TV, my date took his left hand and started massaging his balls. And just like when he had taken his pants off earlier, he sat there, eyes ahead, like it was the most normal thing in the world to be watching TV with a stranger while fiddling with one's sack.

And that, ladies and gentlemen, was when it finally dawned on me.

'Ohhhhh,' my brain realised. 'I'm here for sex. This is a sex thing.'

I figured at that moment I had two choices. I could say thanks but no thanks, and graciously make my exit. Or, I could commit to what this whole Tinder experience had to offer and, well, go with it.

I went with option number two. And as soon as I realised that getting half-naked was not just an odd lifestyle quirk of his, things moved pretty quickly. Before I knew it, half-naked became completely naked, for both of us.

It soon became apparent, though, that Nipple Guy didn't want to get laid so much as he wanted a head job. He kept contorting his body in a way that meant his dick was constantly in my face. He was like a phallic acrobat.

Now, at that point in my life, I had grown enough sexually that I knew when I really didn't want to do something, but I still wasn't great at *saying* when I didn't want to do something. I was of the opinion that if it could be hinted at with a little delicacy, that was far less awkward for everyone involved. So every time he would try and coax my head in that direction, I would halfheartedly stay there for five seconds before making my way back up, hoping that he would get the picture.

But then I would blink, and there'd be a dick in my face again. He was so quick. And we continued playing that weird grown-up version of cat and mouse for about ten minutes, until it reached a bizarre kind of sexual stalemate.

He pushed my head down. I moved my head back up. He pushed my head down. I moved my head back up. We kissed for a bit, and he tried to push my head down again. I moved my head back up. Then he actually got up on his knees and put his dick in my face. So then I got up on *my* knees and started kissing his face again. And just when I was thinking I had won this drunken strategy game of sexual etiquette, he actually *stood up on the bed* and put his dick in my face.

'So this is Tinder,' I thought, as I sat in an unfamiliar room and wondered how much higher this thing could go. 'Playing Jenga with my face and a penis.'

Somehow, I eventually managed to kibosh the head-job idea without ruining the mood (that is, by forcefully pulling him down from his ridiculous standing-on-mattress position), and after that I was ready for it all to be over.

I wasn't really enjoying myself, and he was taking forever. I even faked an orgasm, hoping that maybe he was just waiting for me to finish before he did. But he wasn't taking forever because he had sexual manners. He was taking forever because he still wanted a damn head job. So, getting serious motion sickness from all the thrashing and vodka (and really just wanting to get home to watch *Seinfeld* reruns), I sat up against the head of the bed, opened my mouth and let him fuck it. He came in about eleven seconds. 'Ah,' I thought. 'So all I had to be was a blow-up doll.'

I went to the bathroom to get myself together, and also to try and come up with a good excuse for why I would need to leave immediately. I didn't quite know the etiquette involved. Was he expecting me to stay? How could I leave this place and never come back without seeming rude? I was still trying to figure out what to say when I came out of the bathroom, only to see him fully dressed, looking like he was about to leave.

'Um, I'm really sorry, but I sort of have to go,' he said.

He had to 'go'. From his own house.

'It's my friend, he's going through a really bad break-up, and he really wants me to come over.'

I couldn't believe I was the one getting rejected, when I had just been about to do the rejecting.

'Dude, I was about to leave anyway,' I said, picking up my stuff with an air of dignity not quite befitting someone wearing her underwear backwards.

We gave each other an awkward kiss on the cheek, and I left (after which there's no doubt in my mind he got straight back into bed). I was so pissed that he had been the one to ask me to leave first, that I was determined to be the one to delete him off Tinder first. And as I was sitting in the cab, I realised that it had been almost twenty-four hours exactly since I had signed up to what I now understood was essentially an online sex service. Perfect timing.

I deleted my account. Then I asked the taxi driver to pull over so I could spew.

Starting with the pretty pink penis bow and ending with being fucked in the mouth like a blow-up doll, I'd had ten years of sex completely focussed on what the guy wanted. And after I wiped the excess vomit from the side of my cheek and rolled back into the cab, I let the night wind touch my face as I decided: no more! From that moment on, I was going to make sex about me. I was going to orgasm, and not just by myself in the bathroom. I was going to say no when I wanted and yes when I wanted. I wasn't going to follow ridiculous sex tips just because I was scared of losing a man. I decided in the cab that night that I was going to stop trying to 'do' sexy, and start trying to have sex that I'd actually enjoy.

Sex is messy and funny and weird. You're literally rubbing the parts of your bodies together where your poo and wee comes out. Relax. Remember that it's important that you enjoy it too. Don't do anything you're not comfortable with. And don't ever, ever try to tie a pink bow on some guy's dick.

You will learn how to be a functioning adult, and realise you don't care about being a functioning adult.

When you're twenty-seven years old and realise that you have no clue how to post a letter, it's obvious something has gone very wrong somewhere along the line. I suppose spending a childhood begging my mum to stop drinking and put on some pants, followed by an early adulthood imprisoned by mental-health issues didn't help. But you can't exactly use that as an excuse when an exasperated postal worker looks like they're about to punch you in the face.

I had somehow, against all odds, made it to my late twenties, but there were just some things I had missed along the way. How to post a letter was one of them.

I realised my cluelessness not long after starting at Mamamia, when I was one day required to perform the complex, mind-boggling task of sending an actual physical letter through an actual physical facility. It was all because of some stupid form that needed my stupid *original* signature (trust me, I tried to worm my way around the requirement for weeks) and needed it posted, via snail mail, ASAP.

'Fine,' I thought. 'I'll head to the post office. How hard could it be? I've returned stuff to ASOS before.' ASOS understands that most of their clientele deal exclusively in email, so they make snail mail easy – they give you a sticker with an address on it that you just stick on a bag and give to a person who knocks at your door. What happens from there is a mystery to me. But ASOS emails me when they get the returned items, so I assume it all works. ASOS had lulled me into a false sense of security that sending things in the mail was easy.

I looked in my current envelope, the one the form had come in. They'd included no sticker. Hmmm. There *was* some letter that had an address on it, and instructions for sending my signed form to that address, except there was no '.com' at the end of it so I was confused. I figured I'd just wing it.

When I got to the post office I had a vague idea of what I would need – a stamp and an envelope. But did people actually just buy *one* stamp and *one* envelope? Or was this a bulk-purchasing situation? I took a slow, hesitant walk around the shop. I eventually found envelopes, but no stamps. This stumped me. I figured it would just be easier to line up and have the post office people deal with this complex problem.

When I arrived at the counter the following exchange took place:

Me: Um … I need to post a letter.

Counter Lady: (confused look) There are post boxes outside. You didn't need to line up.

Me: Oh, I know. It's just … I, um …

Counter Lady: (clocking in brain that I am an idiot) Do you not know what to do?

Me: (trying to save face) What?! I *totally* know what to do, it's just, I didn't have any envelopes at home so …

Counter Lady: There are envelopes on the shelf right next to you.

Me: Right, right. So, do you guys sell stamps in singles or …

Counter Lady: (over it, big time) The envelopes are prepaid. See that picture in the corner? That's the stamp.

Me: Ohhhhh, I thought that was just, like, a picture showing you where the stamp should go.

Counter Lady: No. It's not. Do you want to buy the envelope?

I bought the envelope. Then I made my way over to the desk to write the weird .com-free address on the front. Again, I was lost. How am I supposed to know how to format an address without Microsoft Word?

I saw a young guy next to me who looked equally confused. We gave each other an encouraging look, as if to say, 'Don't worry, you're almost through this.' Ten minutes later, after solving the *Good Will Hunting*-esque address formatting riddle, I lined up again so I could send this bloody letter. They need to check it or something, right?

Counter Lady: (about to explode) Is there a problem?

Me: (beaming – extremely proud of myself) Nope! Just want to post my letter!

Counter Lady: Didn't I say before you could just put it in the box outside?

Me: Oh. Right. Don't you need to like, approve it or something?

Counter Lady: (officially over my clueless bullshit) Just give it to me.

I gave it to her.

Counter Lady: (exasperated pause) This address says 'Reply Paid'.

Me: (worried I had failed at cracking the address code) Um … I just copied it straight down. Did I do it wrong?

Counter Lady: No, it's just that – don't you know what 'Reply Paid' means? It means you don't have to pay. You just put it in the envelope they gave you and they pay from their end. Did they send you an empty envelope?

Me: Yeah, but I didn't have any stamps, so I chucked it out.

Counter Lady: You know you could have just posted this without having to come to the post office?

Me: I'm not sure I know anything anymore. Hold me?

I left the letter in her capable hands and contemplated my complete ineptitude at life all the way home. I knew a big part of my problem was that I had no idea how to interact with adults. When it became clear at Mamamia that my writing was popular and I might be a draw to advertisers, my boss Mia tried to take me to some meetings and send me to functions with other 'industry' people. I would spend the entire time in virtual silence, wondering how all the women managed to walk in such high heels without falling over. Then I'd start to worry that I wasn't talking enough, so I'd drop some inevitably awkward TV-related line like, 'So, anyone see that dude get knifed in the balls on *Game of Thrones* this week? That was intense.' I could never tell if they were more perplexed by the fact I had mentioned knifed balls or that I was a 27-year-old woman still using the word 'dude'. I also still carried a backpack, which I could tell caused Mia actual physical pain every time she saw it.

I'd also recently come to realise that I had no clue how to maintain a house. Or, in my case, an apartment that could also be considered a modestly sized walk-in wardrobe by a rich person who buys diamond collars for their purebred teacup bulldogs.

I only realised toilets weren't 'self-cleaning' when the inside of mine started to turn black from too much poo residue. I ignored the problem for as long as I could, and was literally just about to buy a new toilet when I thought I'd check with my sister.

'Oh hey Rhi, by the way …' We'd been on the phone for about half an hour, talking about all the times Mum had called us drunk and told us she hated us that week. 'If your toilet has, you know, stopped cleaning itself, how do you, like, fix that? Or clean it or whatever?'

'Rosie, are you asking me how to clean a toilet?' Rhiannon asked.

'Yes,' I said, hanging my head in shame. 'That is what I am asking.'

'Oh my god. Does that mean you've never cleaned your toilet the whole time you've been living in that apartment? That's fucking gross!'

'Well I thought it just cleaned when you flushed it! Like how you don't have to wash towels because your clean body just keeps them clean when you get out of the shower.'

'Do you not wash your fucking towels? What the fuck, man! That's so disgusting! You are fucking gross, Rosie.'

'But if your body is already clean when you get out of the shower, then why would your towel ever be dirty?'

Rhiannon sighed down the phone. I seemed to make a lot of adults sigh. Unlike me, having a kid when she was nineteen forced Rhiannon to grow up pretty fucking fast. She was scheduling dentist appointments and organising after-school care; I was still drying myself in what were apparently towels covered in mini bacteria colonies. And it had probably been about ten years since I'd been to a dentist, since I'd basically stopped going when government-allocated adults stopped organising it for me.

Rhiannon explained that I needed to get something called 'toilet cleaner' and use that to scrub what was now the almost entirely black coating around the inside of the bowl.

'Wait – I have to put my actual hand inside the actual toilet to clean it?' I said, horrified.

'This coming from the girl who's probably never washed a fucking towel in her life.'

Fair call. I wondered if she would book a dentist appointment for me.

Besides the post office debacle and my complete lack of domestic knowledge (including cooking skills – mine had pretty much never expanded further than Rosie's Chicken Soup and using the oven to heat up my filthy bacteria towels), I realised I really had no clue what it meant to be an adult the day I learned about money. The day I learned about money sent me into a complete and utter existential crisis, the likes of which I hadn't felt since I found myself sitting on top of that dirt mound about to get licked by the girl who smelled like cheese.

I started to make some money (at least, a little bit more than student/retail money), when I realised I had been born with a savant-like skill for writing recaps of a little reality TV show called *The Bachelor*. I never quite understood where the skill came from or why it struck such a chord, but as soon as I started writing a weekly satirical review of the show for Mamamia, my popularity as a writer exploded (something I always felt guilty about, since all I did was watch the show and write down what happened. I mean, come on, it's *The Bachelor*, the jokes pretty much write themselves). The posts started getting hits in the millions. The Mamamia website would break whenever one was published. I was getting recognised in the supermarket. Companies were sending me piles of free stuff. And then came the pay rise. To thank me for being born with the very specific skill of being able to write funny, bitchy jokes about *The Bachelor*, Mamamia gave me a pretty hefty pay rise. And finally having some money made me realise that I have a very limited understanding of where that money was going. Not in a 'Oh whoops, I felt really rich on payday and shouted everyone in the bar' kind of way, but in an actual, logistical 'How does the financial system work?' kind of way. I basically realised I had no freaking clue how banks work. I honestly just assumed that I put my money in the bank and it stayed there until I needed it, in a setting not unlike a vault at Gringotts or Scrooge McDuck's basement.

It's just one of those things I never really thought about, until I thought about it. I'd taken for granted that it all works and the rest of the details were none of my concern. Like how cows turn into burgers, or how getting a manicure is so cheap.

It was a co-worker (unnamed, by request) who made me realise there was yet another damn part of being a functioning adult I knew nothing about. She kicked off my panic by asking,

'When you transfer money online, who physically transfers it? Are there truck drivers or something?'

This immediately made me look up from my desk. Good freaking question. Obviously, I understood that the money isn't shipped around in trucks every time you pay an online bill (sorry, anonymous co-worker – even I knew that much), but when you transfer money online, where does it go? Does online money even exist?

APPARENTLY IT DOESN'T. Upon being informed of this, I proceeded to lose my mind in an 'if a tree falls in the forest/existential crisis/where does space end' kind of way. Here's how the conversation went down, with my incredibly patient and intelligent boss Jamila (who couldn't believe that she'd just caught two employees pondering whether internet money is transferred in trucks):

Me: So hold up, hold up. Is there a physical piece of money for every online piece of money that gets exchanged online?

Jamila: (now questioning my employment status) You mean like an actual piece of plastic with a number on it that one person hands to another person who hands it to the business you're buying something from? No.

Me: But I spend most of my money online. How could it not be real?

Jamila: Well, you're thinking about cash money as if it's something that has inherent worth. It doesn't.

Money is simply a metal or plastic symbol of value. It's a construct that allows us to measure the worth of various goods in comparison to other goods, for the purpose of exchange.

Nowadays Western society tends to use electronic funds. So, yes, there is a finite amount of physical money in circulation but there is no requirement to actually have that sitting in a little box somewhere with your name on it.

Me: So ... wait. *Wait.* You're telling me if I get paid, and then I pay a bill online – that money never existed? It was just a *concept*? What kind of hippy philosophical bullshit is that? It's my money!

Jamila: (losing patience) It did exist, Rosie. It doesn't have to be something that is physically passed around, though. Anyway, even if there was a physical cash representation of every cent you had sitting in the bank – the bank would still be loaning it out. It's not just sitting in a giant – or not so giant – pile somewhere.

Me: But if the money doesn't actually exist, what happens if everyone goes to the bank and wants to get their money out at the same time? Doesn't the bank have a responsibility to make sure everyone's money is available?

Jamila: Well, that's called a run on the bank. Think about what's been happening to the Greek economy in the past few years, or in Argentina a few decades back now. The problem they had is that people were so concerned about the constantly changing value of their money (this is called inflation) that they became distrustful of the banks.

But when huge numbers of people are going to the bank, all trying to withdraw funds at the same time, the bank won't necessarily have the cash on hand to cater for that. So you want to prevent that sort of situation occurring.

Me: *What?* But it's our money! Where is all the money?

Jamila: The bank takes people's money and invests it, or loans it to other people. That's the whole point of a bank.

Me: I didn't give them permission to do that!

Jamila: Well, you did. When you signed up to the bank. And they pay you for letting them use your money while you don't need it; that's why you get interest on your savings. That's the bank basically paying you back for letting them use your money for other things for a period of time.

Me: But how can they invest my money and still have the money in my account when I need it? What if when I go to the bank to withdraw one hundred dollars, they're like, 'Soz, Rosie, your moulah is kind of tied up in Amalgamated Building Society stock right now. We'll let you know how it goes.'

Jamila: (silence)

Me: And what if they lose it! What if they invest my money and lose it? I get like four cents a year in interest on my savings. What if they lose all my money and then are just like, 'Well, we were giving you that four cents a year so … you knew the risks.'

Jamila: Okay, maybe let's try a different tack … Do you remember what happened in the *Mary Poppins* movie? When the little boy started yelling that the bank wouldn't give him his money back? And then all the people thought the bank was in trouble and wanted to withdraw their funds?

Me: (freaking out and ignoring Jamila) So, let me get this straight. Money is just a concept. The money I earn doesn't actually exist. Everybody gives the bank their non-existent money, which is then hypothetically spent on hypothetical investments, which means the bank doesn't actually *look after* everyone's money, they just hypothetically send it away. So if everyone wanted their money at the same time, the bank wouldn't have it. And if the bank invests badly on your behalf and loses everything, the hypothetically non-existent money becomes *actually* non-existent and then it's gone. And too bad, that's it.

Jamila: Um, sort of …

Me: *What?* Our money is resting on a *house of cards*, people. How is this legal?

Jamila: Well, if you want to have your money in a bank, that's what you've agreed to.

Me: Can't I just say to them, 'Look, guys, I want to keep my money here but I don't want you doing anything fancy with it. I'll pay fees and whatever, but I want my physical money here, in a box with my name on it. When I put money in, it's in. When I take money out, it's out. And I'm going to do random cash "spot checks" to make sure it's all here and there hasn't been any funny business.'

Jamila: Well, you're basically describing the equivalent of a shoebox under your mattress.

Me: Well, maybe that's where we're at now.

Jamila: (no words, foetal position, head in hands, tears)

I suppose I was lucky to end up where I did, surrounded by a lot of people who were willing to take the time to explain the ins and outs of adulthood to me. And considering just a few months before starting at Mamamia, I had gotten so drunk I woke up to find that I had shat the bed, I certainly had a lot to learn. A 27-year-old who drinks so much she shits herself is hardly the epitome of adult behaviour. I didn't think it was possible, by the way. I mean, I can understand peeing the bed, because all that takes is for your bladder to get a little too relaxed. But to shit the bed? You've actually got to push that sucker out. At some point in the night, I must have woken up and decided that I couldn't be fucked going to the toilet. At some point during the night, I had weighed up the options and decided that sleeping in my own shit was worth it if it meant I got to stay in bed. I clearly had some growing up to do.

I'd been out drinking with Jacob, and when we drink together we don't mess around; it's usually eight solid hours of wine and bitching about how unjust it is that people we don't like are doing way better at life than us.

I don't remember the moment when I'd had one drink too many, but I do remember I felt completely fine until I went to the toilet. I'm a firm believer in the theory that you never truly know how drunk you are until you're sitting in a toilet cubicle alone. That's when you realise how much the floor is spinning and how you can't get your eyes to focus on the love poem Tammy wrote about Corey's sexy rat's tail in 2002. You go into that cubicle feeling like you could take over the goddamn world, and you leave it barely able to walk. I wobbled over to Jacob and told him the night was over. The 'I'm about to vomit' look on my face meant he knew I was serious. He made sure I got home safely. I crawled into bed and puked on the floor next to me, a problem that I decided to leave for Future Rosie to take care of.

I passed out, in what was certainly one of the more attractive moments of my life.

I woke the next day, mid-afternoon. When my brain realised it had survived the ordeal, it began to focus on the room around me. I was lying virtually exactly as I had fallen asleep – face down on the mattress, naked. The previous evening's spew surprise had dried into the carpet. I looked into the mirror that was adjacent to the bed, thinking that the sight of my hung-over, naked body would at least shame me enough into getting up.

That's when I saw it.

'What the fuck is that?' I thought, as I looked at the little pile of brown positioned perfectly on top of my bum. I was still too hung-over to process what was happening. I was squinting into the mirror, looking at my reflection, trying to figure out what on earth was stuck to my butt cheeks. 'Is that ... is that a *mouse*?' I suddenly panicked, and reached back to slap away whatever was sitting there. That's when reality kicked in. Why, Rosie, would there be a fucking mouse sitting on top of your arse? You *shat* yourself, you fucking gross bitch! You got so drunk last night that *you shat the bed*.

The fact I now had shit on my hand from where I'd tried to slap a mouse away made it abundantly clear that even thinking it could be a mouse was, in fact, ridiculous.

I lay still on the bed, defeated. I was naked, on my stomach. There was shit between my bum cheeks and all over my right hand. There was dried vomit on the floor next to me. And the mirror that ran alongside my bed meant I was forced to look at myself in one of my most shameful moments. I reached over to my phone with my left hand and dialled Rhiannon's number. 'Rhi,' I said, 'I need help.'

'What is it? Where are you?' She sounded a little panicked.

'I'm in my bed, and I'm lying on my stomach, and there's shit all over my arse.'

'What? Whose shit?'

'My shit! Whose shit do you think would be on my arse, you sicko? I got really drunk and shat the bed. And now I'm stuck here because as soon as I turn over or try to get up, it's going to go everywhere.'

I heard nothing but hysterical laughter from the other end of the phone. 'You're on your own, freak,' she said. 'Just get up and try not to touch it.'

'But I already touched it. I thought it was a mouse on my bum.'

'Why would there be a mouse on your bum?'

'You're the one who asked me whose shit it was! I'm hung-over, give me a break.'

'Well, you're going to have to get up some time,' she said, laughing as she hung up.

It took me a good half hour to muster the strength to take care of the situation, all the while promising myself that I would never get that drunk again. Which of course, I have. Many, many times. But I've yet to wake up to another poo surprise, which only suggests growth, in my opinion. I may not know how to cook. I may not know how to carry a conversation with adults that isn't about television. I may not know how to clean a toilet, or how banks work or how to post a letter. But I've only ever pooped once from being drunk. And that seems pretty grown-up to me.

You will become an Anti-Cool Girl.

I'm currently sitting in a blanket fort that I built around my TV, drinking vodka and pretending that I don't have a book deadline. I haven't showered in three days, partly because I don't want to leave the blanket fort, but mostly because my cat has done a big shit in the bathroom and I can't be bothered cleaning it up.

I'm scared to come out. I'm scared to come out of a freaking blanket fort. I'm feeling overwhelmed, and tired, and I just figured out how to get Netflix to play on my TV, so it's really difficult to muster the motivation to leave this safe, warm, vodka-filled happy place.

I'm twenty-eight, I'm not wearing pants, there's about seven different food stains on my t-shirt and I'm hiding in a blanket fort in my living room. And you know what? I don't give a shit.

Sometimes I just need to sit in a blanket fort for a while with some fucking vodka. And it took me a long time, but I'm finally okay with that. I'm an often glorious, currently pantsless, cheese-loving mess, who will never, ever be cool enough to handle life without the occasional fort-related breakdown. That's just me.

I spent a lifetime struggling to understand why I wasn't a cool kid, constantly wondering just what I was missing. From my early days trying to hide my poo pants from my sister's friends, to my later days doing drugs and pretending to enjoy sex with boys who were terrible at it, I've always been so fixated on trying to impress everyone around me, trying to be what I thought I was meant to be. But I spent so much time attempting to crack the damn code that would finally get me on the inside that I never stopped to ask myself if that was actually where I wanted to be.

It wasn't until I found myself there that I realised it wasn't.

Not too long ago, for a very brief and exhausting moment, I found myself on the inside looking out. I was surrounded by glamour and famous people and lots and lots of air kissing, and I ended up sitting on the side of the road by myself, eating a taco in a ball gown.

After becoming a fairly popular writer on Mamamia, my editors decided to send me on a trip to Los Angeles to cover the 'G'day USA' gala, which is basically just an excuse for all the famous US-based Aussies to get together and get pissed on someone else's dime. I had to go to a bunch of parties, swan about with famous people and then write about the experience when I got home.

I really thought my life had officially come full circle. I was the phoenix rising from the ashes, the flower growing out of the mud etc etc etc blah blah blah. The little girl who hid in her room memorising lines from sitcoms while her mum drunk-cried over Elton John music downstairs was GOING TO HOLLYWOOD, BITCHES. I had made it.

When I first saw the Hollywood sign from my balcony, I cried. After everything, after every god damn thing, I was standing in a plush Beverly Hills hotel room, looking at the Hollywood sign, and I was there as a *paid writer*. I got a taxi to take me to the Kodak Theatre, where the Oscars are held. I walked up to the doors and pressed my palms against them, thinking of every speech I had ever planned to give on that stage since I was five years old. I'm sure thousands of girls do the same thing every year. I'm surprised there wasn't an official 'Look How Far You've Come' line for everyone who wants to take a photo with their eyes closed, while they smile wistfully with their hands pressed against the door of the Kodak Theatre. It was a cliché moment, definitely. But holy shit, it was a good moment.

Lifelong dream-fulfilling out of the way, I had to get down to the business of being an impossibly cool person in my impossibly cool new job. I had 'made it', you see. I needed to get dressed up and go to parties and take selfies with the beautiful people. If only I had known, all those years ago, when I was being laughed at while my mum wiped shit from my thighs, that one day I would be paid to hang out with celebrities and write about it. If only I had known, while being tortured by Wayne at The College, that I was going to become a total insider. If only I had known, every time I felt weird and awkward and out of place, that one day I would reach the absolute top rung of the cool ladder.

If only I had known, that once I got there, I would really, really hate it.

John Travolta kissed me on the cheek. Jacki Weaver laughed at one of my jokes. Kylie Minogue sang a private concert next to some hotel pool. I ordered a drink while standing at the bar next to Geoffrey Rush. I posted pictures on Instagram that made it look like I was having the time of my life.

But I was miserable. I was so fucking miserable. Those few days of fancy celebrity parties in LA were a few of the most uncomfortable days of my life. I don't know why I assumed that once I was finally on the 'inside', that once I was finally a cool kid, it would all make sense to me. None of it made sense to me. I may have finally been accepted by the cool kids, but I still felt weird and awkward and out of place. And on my last night in LA, I realised why.

It's because I *am* weird and awkward and out of place. I was never cool because I was never meant to be cool, and standing at one of the most exclusive parties in LA that night, I looked around the room and realised I didn't *want* to be either. Being cool is exhausting, and after just a few days, I'd had enough.

I needed air. I needed to stop pretending I enjoyed small talk and that my heels were comfortable. I needed to eat something that wasn't a wanky canapé. I needed to be somewhere that wasn't playing music so loud I couldn't think. I just needed to get the hell out of that party.

So I left. In my ball gown, with my face made up and my hair looking fucking fabulous, I walked out of the coolest situation I had ever found myself in. I walked away from the party I had spent my entire life trying to get into. I wandered the streets of LA until I found a food truck on the side of the road. I ordered a taco and ate it while sitting on the kerb, and I had never felt more relieved in my life. That kerb was exactly where I was supposed to be.

I'm weird and awkward and out of place, and sometimes blanket forts and taco-kerbs are just more my style. Realising that is what finally gave me permission to stop trying so hard.

After that night, I realised that as soon as you stop listening to what everyone else wants from you, and start listening to what *you* want from you, your life will get easier. There is nothing more liberating than accepting who you are, shit mishaps, taco-kerbs, blanket forts and all. It may not be cool, it may not be perfect, but it's you, and every experience you've had in your life has played a part in creating that. There were times my life was rough, but all of it led to me walking out of that fancy party to get a taco, because I finally realised that after everything I'd been through, the only person I needed to impress was me. And sitting on that kerb, eating that delicious pocket of cheese and meat, I was pretty damn impressed with myself. I finally cracked the code I was meant to crack all along: being cool is all about compromising who you are. Being anti-cool is about accepting it. Accepting it, owning it, laughing at it and loving it. I was never meant to be cool. I was meant to be anti-cool.

That fancy LA party just wasn't me. You know what *is* me? This:

1. I refuse to wax my pubes. There is honestly no grand feminist reasoning behind this choice, it's just that ripping hair out of your vagina really fucking hurts. I did it once, for a boy, and was so traumatised by the experience that I never did it again. Also, pubes just don't really bother me, and if they ever bothered a man I was with, I would ask him to kindly step away from my special place.
2. I still have stuffed toys on my shelves.
3. I've accepted that I'm not great at being 'sexy'. Flannelette pyjamas and fanny farts are both words that I'd use to describe a typical sexual experience with me. And I like that.
4. I'll never be afraid of being alone again. There are worse things than being alone, like ... being with a man who treats

you badly. Being single can be scary, but it also means you get to drink wine in your underpants and take your laptop to the toilet.

5. I've only vacuumed twice this year.

6. I won't do any sex stuff that makes me uncomfortable. Emotionally or physically. Bum stuff is out. A guy tried once, and I reflexively kicked him in the balls, so venture there at your own risk. Also …

7. I won't pretend that I've orgasmed when I haven't. I have faked many an orgasm in my time. Then I realised sex wasn't just about him feeling like a sex god. In fact, and this may sound crazy, but sex is actually kind of pointless unless you also enjoy it. As soon as I realised that, I wouldn't say I'd climaxed unless I had. You are entitled to orgasm. They may have to work a little harder but … well, I couldn't give a fuck, to be honest.

8. I've made peace with my mental health. My anxiety will always be with me, and that's fine. It sometimes means I have to slow my life down. It sometimes means I'll hide in the bathroom at work and have a panic attack. It sometimes means I'll sit in a blanket fort until I feel safe enough to come out. I have to take medication every day and I'll probably always be in therapy. But accepting it has made me a better person.

9. I lied. I've only vacuumed once this year.

10. I don't let my appearance have anything to do with anyone but me. Every choice I make about the way I look is to make me happy, not so a man will feel good about having me on his arm. My hair? For me. My make-up (or, usually, lack thereof)? For me. The clothes I wear? For me. My body? For me.

11. I can't cook and I have no interest in learning how. Anyone who ventures into my home must be willing to accept a thoughtfully ordered take-out meal or some variation of a toasted sandwich. Also, I never put food in my oven — it's for heating up towels.

12. I have the alcohol tastes of a fifteen-year-old girl. I need all my alcoholic beverages to be sweet and bubbly. I don't like beer. Never have, never will. Some other girl can chug down with the boys — I'm perfectly happy with my sparkling wine, thank you very much. And it's usually the cheapest one, because I can't taste the difference. I may not understand the 'woody undertones' of an expensive red, but everything I drink tastes like a glorious fruit cocktail, so suck it.

13. I will never let anyone convince me that I'm not 'fuckable'. If you like to fuck, you are fuckable. It's that simple.

14. I have accepted that going out is for chumps. TV is my one true love. There was a brief period there where I tried to be 'down' with the kids. I went to the clubs. I took drugs. I hung out in places with music so loud that my ears would ring for

days. Then I realised that it was the worst. I like soft lighting, yummy wine and a good TV show (and if you're lucky, I may even put on pants).

15. I refuse to waste my time loving someone who doesn't love me.

16. I have forgiven my parents. They did the best they could, while both dealing with tragic struggles of their own. And they gave me the gift of a brilliant brain, which I'll always be thankful for.

17. I'm scared that if I learn to drive, I'll crash while singing a Disney song.

18. Yes, I'm twenty-eight and I just admitted that I don't know how to drive.

19. I feel like a fraud ninety-five percent of the time. I literally have no idea what I'm doing, and I cannot believe people pay me to write the words I have written when I still sleep with a teddy bear.

20. I need to be able to fart in front of my boyfriends. Non-negotiable.

21. Although I'm terrified almost all of the time, I really think I'm doing okay. After everything, after every damn thing, I'm actually kind of doing okay.

So there you have it. That's all my ... stuff, embarrassing or otherwise, on the table. I accept it and I own it and I'm proud of it. I'll only ever change that list if I'm the one who isn't happy with it. I'm not trying to be cool anymore – my list changes for nobody but me.

This isn't some grand life philosophy. There are no rules. I don't give a fuck what direction people lean in or what plan they follow or if they secretly love eating cheese in the bath. Just try to love yourself enough that you never feel like you have to pretend to be something that you're not. Sit on the kerb eating a taco, or stay at the fancy party until 4am, if that's what you want. Just make sure it's what YOU want.

It doesn't mean life will always be perfect, but it does mean that it will always be real.

And that's it. After everything I went through, everything I survived, the most important lesson I learned only came after having an epiphany while eating a taco in a ball gown. Do with that lesson what you will.

Now please excuse me while I climb out of this blanket fort, put on some pants, and try to keep my life halfway together.

Acknowledgments

My glorious publisher Catherine Milne, you somehow managed to only very politely prod me along when I was missing deadlines and probably giving you stress-related heart palpitations. You have walked me through the process of writing my first book with the patience and nurturing that I needed. Here's to many, many more.

Kathy Hassett, James Kellow, Shona Martyn and the entire team at HarperCollins. I feel so lucky to be working with all of you.

James, thank you for being my blanket fort when I needed it most. This book actually may not have been finished without your dweeby excel skills.

Gretel Killeen, you snuck me drinks in the Qantas lounge and gave me the exact advice I needed to hear. It helped more than you know. Thank you.

Mia Freedman and Jamila Rizvi, thank you both for changing the course of my life. You are brilliant women and

I'm so privileged to know both of you. May the battle to be my mentor rage on. And to every single person who I've worked with at the Mamamia Women's Network, I consider you family. Please don't pass me the nipple ball if it looks like I've got nothing.

All the boys I ever dated: I faked orgasms with some of you and not others, so have fun working that out.

Antonio Sergi and Jacob Stanley, for being the brothers I never had and the most fabulous, supportive, wine-drinking best friends a girl could ever ask for.

Allira and Mohammed, sorry you don't get mentioned in this book. Please proceed to do many embarrassing things that I can spend a lifetime writing about.

And finally, Mama. Thank you for calling me darling and hugging me like nobody else does. I love you.